SPARKING GREATNESS

Harnessing the Power of Inspiration
to Lead Boldly and Live Fully

DANIELLE B. BALDWIN

BRIGHT HOLLOW PRESS
San Diego, California

Published by Bright Hollow Press
brighthollowpress.com

Book Design: Clarity Designworks

ISBN 979-8-9931227-1-7 (paperback)
ISBN 979-8-9931227-0-0 (hardcover)
ISBN 979-8-9931227-2-4 (ebook)

Learn more at sparkinggreatness.com.

For my family, my constant spark

CONTENTS

INTRODUCTION

THE SPARK

A conversation with a coaching client sparked the question that led to this book. I was talking with Brenton Sullivan, CEO and founder of FieldLevel, a sports platform connecting athletes, coaches, and teams with opportunity. It was the first summer of the COVID-19 pandemic, and many leaders were touching base with their employees frequently while we were all in lockdown. Brenton described the check-in meetings they'd recently had in their organization. Each employee met with their manager and then had a follow-up meeting with Brenton. He'd noticed a perplexing pattern with those meetings based on employee feedback.

"D, it's the craziest thing. I'm trying to get my head around it," Brenton told me during our coaching session.

"I'm super curious—tell me."

"We had individual meetings with every employee last week. At the end of every meeting, we asked employees the same three questions: if they understood their role, the current state of the company, and in general, how they were feeling."

"Those sound like the right questions."

"Totally. The questions worked. So here's where it gets weird. When employees finished meeting with their direct manager, they answered the questions 'Yes,' 'Yes,' and 'Motivated.'"

"Got it."

"So then I met with every employee and ended the meeting with the same three questions. You know what they said?"

"Something different?"

"The first two questions were answered the same—with yeses. But for the last one, to a person, the employees mentioned that they felt 'inspired.' Why do you think that is?"

I took a sip of coffee to buy some time to think. I was stumped. "Wow. I could hazard some guesses, but I'm not 100 percent sure about that."

"I know. I mean, what is inspiration anyway?"

And that, my friends, is when the inspiration lightning bolt hit me—sitting at my kitchen table, midmorning in summer of 2020.

The immediate question both Brenton and I were left with was *why*. Why was it that these employees felt different from one conversation to the next? What did Brenton say that was so different from what their managers and directors told them? The more we talked about it, the more we were both curious about how Brenton and his leaders could more consistently inspire the team, knowing that an inspired team was more productive, more engaged, and more aligned than a less inspired one. If we could figure it out, then we could make it repeatable, and in an era with high turnover and low employee retention, this could have a tremendous impact on the culture and the growth of the company.

The conversation also brought to light questions about motivation and inspiration. When, as leaders, do we want to motivate vs. inspire? How do we do each of those well? What is the key to unlocking inspiration in our employees and how do we motivate them?

As these questions swirled in my head, I came across the real kicker—it's all fine and good to determine when and how to motivate and inspire our employees, but how is that even possible when we as leaders are exhausted, burned out, and neither motivated nor inspired ourselves?

After all, we're living in unprecedented times, especially for leaders. We've never lived in an era quite like this one—politically, economically, ecologically, sociologically, and medically. Change is happening at a lightning-fast clip, on top of the regular seasons of life we go through: parents growing older, reorganizations at work, our kids and grandkids growing up and moving out, our social circle shifting or shrinking, our bodies aging—maybe not as gracefully as we might like. All of those have an impact on us. They take a toll.

Even for those of us who have conquered great challenges in our lives, we can reach a place where we feel like we're treading water in the middle of the ocean without land in sight. It's difficult. And in these times, we can lose our light of inspiration.

With all this in mind, I realized I needed to start at the beginning and answer basic questions about inspiration.

As a society, we throw around the term "inspiration"—but what is inspiration, really? How does it work in our bodies? Are there universal truths about what we all find inspiring? How is inspiration different from motivation? How are they the same? If inspiration, by nature, is fleeting, how can we capture it? If we can't predict when it appears, can we at least set the stage for inspiration?

Once we have a good idea of exactly what inspiration and motivation are and how they work, we need to start bringing more inspiration into our own lives before we can hope to inspire those around us. Other than differentiating motivation from inspiration, we'll focus the rest of the book on inspiration alone.

There are six parts to this book, each designed to build upon the last. In part 1, we explore what inspiration is, why it matters, and how it differs from motivation, laying the groundwork for everything that follows.

In part 2, we'll look at overcoming burnout and overwhelm. As the old saying goes, "We need to fill our own cups before we can fill the cups of others." It's far more difficult to inspire or motivate when we lack our own inspiration and motivation. In parts 3 through 5, we'll cover the three distinct pillars that set the stage for inspiration. Each chapter in here includes practical exercises: one set for you as the leader to work on personally, and another set for you to use with your team.

I had an opportunity while writing this book to use many of these exercises. Ironically, it's entirely possible to become both unmotivated and uninspired while writing a book on both topics. The good news—both motivation and inspiration can come back. We'll cover some exercises and techniques to invite them both back into the room.

Part 6 takes us to the framework for inspirational narrative. We know not only from research but from our own experience the unique power of story to motivate and inspire people toward positive change. I've identified five core elements of stories that truly inspire. We'll explore examples of each element and examine familiar stories so you can see the complete framework in action, giving you the tools to craft stories that inspire others.

If you've read all of this and still wonder if you're in the right place, this book is written for leaders who recognize themselves in this story: those who have lost their spark and are struggling to reignite their own inspiration, as well as leaders who want to more consistently inspire their teams.

Whether you're a CEO like Brenton, a middle manager stretched thin, or a team lead looking to create more engagement, this book will help you understand and harness the power of inspiration both for yourself and those you lead.

Inspiration is incredibly powerful and can often change our direction in life. It brings us extraordinary amounts of clarity. We move closer to our life's purpose and closer to that future version of ourselves that we know we can be.

Here's the most beautiful thing about inspiration—an inspired life can start at any moment. While this book will give you the tools to set the stage for more frequent inspiration in your own life and help you inspire others, since the dawn of human history, people have been inspired without knowing how it works.

We can catch the fireflies of inspiration at any time. The life we've dreamed of, the big idea, the solution, the happily ever after (if that's what we want)—it's waiting to unfold. We can swim in pools of starlight and dream in fields of wildflowers. We can sail across the sun, float amongst the stars. That's what's so exciting about inspiration—in a heartbeat, the spark of the life you've always dreamed of is within reach.

I hope this book is as inspirational as it is motivational. May it bring an abundance of each to your life and to those around you.

PART 1

UNDERSTANDING INSPIRATION

1

I KNOW IT WHEN I FEEL IT

You know that moment when you feel a spark or have a flash of lucidity? Maybe you're standing in the shower, working the shampoo into a healthy lather, thinking about nothing in particular when—BAM— the answer to that nagging work problem pops into your brain. Or you're jogging along, podcast in your ears and the steady beat of your feet on the ground and—BAZINGA—you suddenly know exactly what to say in that conversation you've been dreading. You could be at a conference, listening to a key-note speaker who completely changed the direction of their lives and achieved a dream that seemed impossible, and then you suddenly have a burst of clarity. You're able to instantaneously make connections and insights you couldn't see before. You think to yourself, "I could do this too." You can start a nonprofit. You can pursue your love of painting. You can learn a new language. Whatever has pulled at the edges of your hopes and dreams is within reach. You feel excited, illuminated, confident.

That's inspiration.

Inspiration has been a critical part of human evolution for over a thousand years. Inspiration as a concept can be traced back to as early as 1000 B.C., where we see it appear in religious texts across Buddhism, Christianity, Islam, and Judaism to describe the divine influence and connection between humans and God. Inspiration has guided our organizations, communities, religions, cultures, and families for centuries. Flashes of inspiration have driven great advances in science, technology, changes in social structures, and what we thought was possible for the human body to achieve.

When we think of inspiration, we may envision luminaries, like Leonardo da Vinci creating the first drawing for an airplane or a helicopter, or Steve Jobs creating the Apple 1 computer, or Rosa Parks igniting desegregation in public transit, or Roger Bannister breaking the four-minute mile. Over and over we hear stories of inspired visionaries who changed the world. When we study the early years of people who made these movements or achievements possible, we often find that they were inspired through interactions with other people to find their passion or dreams.

Paul McCartney was first inspired to be a singer-songwriter by listening to and watching Elvis Presley.

Vincent van Gogh was inspired by the Impressionists and Neo-Impressionists to create some of the most well-known paintings in the world.

For every turning point that changed history and drove innovation in science, or art, or business, there are smaller instances of no less importance—everyday experiences that inspire us. You might read a story in the news about the nonprofit leader who works tirelessly to support the local homeless community. You may know a former gang member who now works with other gang members to transition out of gang life. You might be in line at the office supply store behind a middle school teacher with her arms full of school supplies she's paying for out of her own pocket.

In my line of work, I'm lucky enough to hear these types of stories all the time. Remember Brenton from the introduction? I asked him to describe one of his most powerful experiences of inspiration. He tells the story of the moment he had the idea for his company. He was sitting in an entrepreneurship class at the University of Southern California and staring off into space. He was tired and mentally spent. Brenton knew he had to write a business plan as part of his thesis but had no idea what he should focus on. He'd spent hours debating the pros and cons of different industries, products, and services. He'd had conversations with family, friends, and classmates. He thought about it at the gym, while he drove to and from school, while he watched TV. It had been taking up most of his conscious brain space for weeks, from the minute he woke up to the minute he fell asleep as he went around and around considering potential business ideas, never quite landing on "the one." He'd tried everything to solve the issue logically, and nothing was working.

That day in class, as Brenton sat exhausted, frustrated, and out of ideas, a serial entrepreneur came in to speak. He told the students, "I know most of you are trying to figure out what to write your business plan about or how to decide what business to start. The best advice I can give you is to focus on a problem that is important to you personally. It's better to start a business when you have a passion for solving that problem."

And that was it.

Instantly, Brenton knew. He'd had a lot of trouble extending his athletic career. While he loved baseball and had been a talented catcher in high school, he had difficulty continuing to play baseball into college. The keys to making the transition from high school to college athletics, aside from skills and talent, are access and visibility. He hadn't been able to get in front of the scouts and coaches from schools that may have recruited him because he didn't know how to access them. But what if there was a platform that could connect high school players to college coaches? What if any high school athlete, regardless of circumstance, who wanted to continue to play sports in college had a better shot at doing so because they could get in front of hundreds of coaches around the country?

Brenton describes his flash of inspiration as feeling grounded and deeply connected to the idea. At the same time, he said he felt like he was floating, like all the fog had cleared and everything was extraordinarily clear. He felt no doubt, no hesitation. He said he felt euphoric. It was a sense of clarity and affirmation felt deep in his bones.

Regardless of where or when these moments happen, they fill us with a flash of light. We might feel an openness in our chest, a sense of joy and warmth. We may feel euphoric, like Brenton did. The feeling of inspiration is transcendent, meaning it allows us to rise above the ordinary and gives us the ability to see beyond what we've been able to see in the past. These lightbulb moments provide a deep sense of clarity and perspective. It's like looking all the way through to the bottom of a swiftly moving creek, seeing every rock, every stone, every fish.

Sounds pretty good, right?

What's fascinating about inspiration is that it can strike us at any time. We can be in the car or in the dentist's chair. We can be standing on the side of the field at our kid's soccer game or jogging through the neighborhood after work. We can be sitting with a friend in their backyard drinking a cup of coffee or folding laundry in the living room. When we're alone and the insight hits us, it's like a flash of clarity comes out of nowhere when we least expect it.

Then there are the sparks of inspiration that remind us of an old dream, like becoming a writer or an entrepreneur. Inspiration hits when we see a successful writer or hear an entrepreneur speak. Their story reminds us that we, too, can do what they did. We learn something new about them. "Oh, he didn't start his first company until he was forty-five? So it's not too late for me?" Inspiration can seem like breaking conventional norms, but more often, it's breaking the limitations that we set for ourselves.

Sometimes inspiration gives us a vision or an idea that we've never thought of. We've never picked up a paintbrush before but decide to take a watercolor class with our Aunt Madge. And when we're in the class, it feels natural. Something about this new activity entices us, and we might find that we're pretty good at it even though we've never done it before. We feel drawn to water-color painting. It's an entirely new world, and we want to explore it. This is an example of being inspired to do something that isn't already in our world.

You might get an idea for a project that suddenly turns into the nonprofit you've always wanted to start. Or maybe a question you hear someone answer during a podcast that you're listening to on your commute home spurs you to start a short story that's been brewing just outside your conscious mind.

Inspiration often arrives in boring places, during activities we do every day. It might show up as we feel the water pouring over our heads in the shower, or pull a weed from the garden, or listen to an old playlist while we're stuck in traffic, or sit on our front stoop watching the cars go by.

Sometimes inspiration finds us in nature, in the rattle of aspen leaves, the way the late-afternoon light ripples across a meadow, in the twinkling periwinkle of dusk. It envelopes us as the sun rises over a misty mountaintop, the glow of moonlight shimmers off the ocean's surface, or a meteor shower streaks across the sky. Inspiration can strike as a fireworks display blooms in the summer night or while we watch the world go by from the window seat of an airplane.

Sometimes moments of inspiration happen when we gather with others or participate in a favorite activity. We can feel it during the first chords of our favorite rock song or the ending notes of a beloved aria, from the instant the curtain goes up on opening night, or that breathless pause at the top of a roller coaster or a ski slope. Inspiration can strike the first time you laced up a new pair of sneakers as a kid, convinced they made you faster than anyone in the world. It might show up as you open a brand-new journal, ready to start your self-care journey or write a novel. It can happen watching your baseball hero hit a home run.

In these instances, we're front and center to the world around us. Instead of jumping up and down in front of us, frantically waving their hands, our thoughts dawdle behind us, criss-crossing the path, until suddenly they sprint forward, gasping for air, with "the" idea, leaving us illuminated and breathless.

We use the word *inspiration* without really thinking about it. For years, psychologists have struggled to define the concept. Was it awe, hope, creativity, motivation? Regardless, the more we understand it, the better we can harness it. Inspiration is a real and powerful force, and it can be sparked.

Inspiration, as defined by the Latin root *inspirer*, is "to breathe or blow into." We blow on an ember to start a fire, a musical instrument to create sound, balloons to give them shape. The most compelling aspect about when we "breathe into something" is that we are breathing life into it. We are creating.

Modern definitions of inspiration focus on animating and exalting, influencing, and "to bring about, or to incite."

In essence, inspiration is a kind of spark. It lights something up in us, whether that's a dream, idea, or vision, and it moves us. We feel a jolt of clarity, or a breath of possibility. It's brief, but its effect can last a lifetime.

Two psychologists, Todd Thrash and Andrew Elliot, laid the foundation for the psychological study of inspiration. Thrash is internationally recognized for his work on the scientific study of inspiration, including his creation of the widely used "Inspiration Scale." Elliot is an award-winning researcher who focuses on motivation, achievement, and social connection. In their joint 2003 study, they separate inspiration into three core elements:

» Sparked spontaneity

» Transcendence

» Approach motivation (being motivated by positive things, like excitement about a possible reward or the desire to achieve something good)

Sparked Spontaneity

Sparked spontaneity speaks to the sudden and fleeting nature of inspiration. It's why so many of our analogies for inspiration are centered around images such as sparks, lighting bolts, or fireworks. It's the BAM! idea in the shower, the BAZINGA! moment during a run. But don't confuse the short-lived experience of inspiration with short-term effect. The spark can fuel real, long-term change.

Transcendence

Inspiration lifts us out of the day-to-day. We zoom out and gain greater perspective. In that perspective shift, we're reminded that there's more possibility, more meaning, more potential. Suddenly the thing that felt out of reach is within arm's length. It feels doable. While the challenge may not shrink, we grow in our belief that we can handle it.

Approach Motivation

Inspiration goes beyond a feeling. When we're "inspired to" do something, we take action. Inspiration is like putting on a pair of glasses. The vision that had been fuzzy and hard to articulate, inspiration brings into focus. Inspiration calls us forward with energy and often urgency. Whether sparked by hope or hardship, joy or injustice, approach motivation turns insight into action.

Together, these three components offer important insights into inspiration. It's not just about you connecting with your best ideas. It's about suddenly connecting you with your greatest self, a glimpse of the highest version of yourself, potentially your life's purpose. And it makes you want to take the next step toward the goal, the dream, the vision. Even if that step is difficult, you see the possibilities, and in that instant, your potential feels limitless.

2

WHY INSPIRATION MATTERS

To illustrate why inspiration matters, let's meet Sam. Sam was frustrated because he was unable to scale the manufacturing business he had inherited from his father.

Nothing was wrong, exactly. The company was profitable, employee turnover was low, and customer retention was high. But despite his best efforts to grow the company, it sat at the same revenue and profit numbers year after year. Sam knew the company was capable of more.

When he took a closer look at his organization, reviewing sales and marketing, finance, HR and hiring practices, and even his IT infrastructure, he initially diagnosed his biggest issue as an operations problem—more specifically, a workflow issue. Sam believed he needed to streamline his operations to scale efficiently and hesitantly agreed to overhaul the framework his father had put in place decades earlier.

Sam worked with his team during the next several months to redesign and implement the new processes on the production floor. He and the leadership team put the finishing touches on it, and they implemented everything.

And you know what happened? Very little. The updated approach made only a small impact on productivity and the slightest shift in revenue. Sam and his leadership team were perplexed. They'd addressed what they thought were the biggest problems creating bottlenecks on the floor, put in the time to create new solutions, and executed them well. The lack of results caused Sam to doubt the efficiency of the new framework and he began to make small tweaks reverting to some of their old processes, despite his team's objections.

Before Sam could go all the way back to the old way of doing things, the team convinced him that maybe, just maybe, they needed an outside perspective with additional expertise. Sam brought in a consultant specializing in operational optimization. This consultant reviewed their work and validated their progress, then further refined the methodology and worked with Sam and the team to implement it.

Still nothing. The team was excited and on board. The new structure was in place . . . mostly. Even though he'd agreed to the changes in public, in private Sam was continuing to tweak and change things back to the way they'd been.

It didn't make any sense. Sam recognized that there was a bottleneck in operations, had used all the logic in the world, all the experts and linear next steps to solve his scalability problem, and yet something still wasn't working.

So he sat down with his coach and they dug a little deeper. They decided to bring it to Sam's peer advisory board.

Focusing on logic—the process itself—wasn't going to solve Sam's scalability issue. He could have brought in every operational optimization expert in the world, and nothing would have changed. His peer group could have made all kinds of suggestions about efficiency and utilization rates. But they didn't. Instead, the group focused on Sam. With the help of his peers, Sam realized that his fear of change and failure was holding him back. He'd taken over the company from his father, and part of him deep down worried that by changing processes, the company would fail and he'd disappoint his dad.

Sam realized that his fear of disappointing his father was limiting his ability to scale his company.

In that instant, Sam had complete and total clarity. Not only could he see his roadblocks and limiting beliefs but also the true potential of his organization and what it was capable of. With that shift in perspective, Sam was able to stay the course on the changes, and those changes allowed the organization to double its revenues year over year.

In a moment of inspiration like Sam had, anything feels possible. We can imagine a different version of ourselves, we see the world is our oyster, we can see the next step to becoming anything we want.

Inspiration can shift your perspective, from how you look at your immediate surroundings to how you see the world. Its impact is tremendous, and as a result, it can change your life. But the question remains: Do we really need it? How important is inspiration in your organization or in your day-to-day life?

Inspiration is not a necessity. Not by any means. We can go through life with not even a nanosecond of inspiration and live a perfectly good life. Our organization can exist and be profitable. Employees and customers will stay. The company can grow and thrive.

Everything in our lives can exist in this steady hum with absolutely nothing wrong.

Let's go back to Sam. Sam's company wasn't losing money. His employees and customers were happy. He could have kept the business as it was and retired happily. But he had the sense that the company was capable of more.

In that wallop of an "aha" moment, Sam could see it. Not only a potential for the organization beyond what he'd thought possible but also a higher, more evolved, maybe even a little more divine version of himself. He saw the leader he could be.

Inspiration brings us, in many instances, closer to greatness. It brings us joy and purpose.

Inspiration is a funny thing. We know it strikes at random—in the shower, in the car, or sometimes at 2:00 a.m. when you should be sleeping. It seems like a no-brainer in our personal lives. But I wanted to know where most people experience inspiration. So I conducted a survey of over 250 leaders. And only 1.2 percent of respondents found inspiration in the workplace. Only 1.2 percent!

Here's the bad news: People are wildly uninspired at work.

Here's the good news: As my Grandpa Ray used to say, "You can't fall out of a ditch."

While we know that we can plod along fine at work without any change, below are four benefits we see both as leaders and for our employees/organization as a whole when we inspire ourselves and others:

1. Higher levels of creativity and curiosity, leading to more efficient problem-solving

2. Greater vision/perspective

3. Elevated performance

4. Deeper connection to the cause, purpose, or mission

Higher Levels of Creativity and Curiosity

Inspiration sparks new ways to solve problems.

Sometimes in business, I encounter the outdated belief that creativity, curiosity, and inspiration only belong in the "softer" sides of business, like marketing, PR, or HR. I've heard time and time again that "business problems should be solved by process and theory, applied science and logic." And while those are great ways to solve challenges and obstacles we find in our organizations, they're not the only ways.

Perhaps you've heard of the left brain being logical and the right brain being creative? Although that theory has been debunked (or at the very least, is a great oversimplification), we're going to borrow it anyway as a helpful metaphor. Imagine both sides of our brains are sitting at desks in a classroom and our consciousness is standing up front as the teacher. If the classroom mimics what we typically see in business, our consciousness constantly calls on our left brains, while our right brains slouch in those molded plastic chairs wondering when they'll get a chance to participate. What's wrong with that? What happened to "If it ain't broke, don't fix it?"

Nothing. As I mentioned earlier, an inspired state isn't necessary. Plenty of people go through their lives without feeling a deep sense of inspiration or perhaps not even wanting to feel it.

Inspiration is not required.

But here's why inspiration is important. It breathes life into our organizations, our ideas, our passion, our dreams, and our lives. Inspiration sparks our bursts of genius. When we use our traditional ways of approaching opportunities or challenges, when we zoom in on our issues, when we bust out the microscope or magnifying glass, we constrict. We put on blinders. We may not see the issue in its entirety. In the worst case, we may be solving the wrong issue or challenge entirely. Assuming we are solving the proper issue, using the traditional ways can lead to more of the same thinking, our solutions can lack creativity, and they often fail to challenge the status quo.

An inspired state allows us to remove the proverbial blinders and to more easily tap into our creativity. Inspiration sparks curiosity. That curiosity feeds into creative thinking, which in turn can cycle into an inspired state. This can create an upward cycle of energy. Maya Angelou said it best, "You can't use up creativity. The more you use, the more you have," and we see this in the powerful loop between inspiration, curiosity, and creativity.

Greater Vision and Perspective

Let's go back to Sam. In his flash of inspiration, Sam felt a deep sense of clarity and vision. His perspective shifted dramatically as a result. He had a grander vision for his company and a different perspective on what his problems were, where they were coming from, and how to solve them. Remember the psychological definition of inspiration mentioned earlier? Transcendence, a core element of inspiration, refers to that feeling of elevation and, as a result, shifting our perspective.

Elevated Performance

We know that inspiration creates a powerful loop with curiosity and creativity, but how does this impact performance?

Bain & Company conducted a study in 2015 that placed employees into three categories of needs similar to Maslow's hierarchy (see illustration on page 62). "Satisfied employees" populate the bottom tier. These employees have their basic needs covered; they feel mentally and physically safe at work, are valued and rewarded, and have the tools and the time to complete their duties and tasks. "Engaged employees" occupy the next tier. Engaged employees feel they are part of an incredible team, able to learn and grow, have autonomy, and most important, understand how they make a difference in the organization.

"Inspired employees" form the top tier of the pyramid. An inspired employee reports feeling inspired not only by the company's mission but also by its leadership.

The difference between the three groups of employees was described in the study this way: When a group of satisfied employees encounter a wall at work, they'll meet to discuss a solution. Engaged employees will look around for a ladder. Inspired employees will run through the wall.

How does this show up in productivity? According to the study, inspired team members were 250 percent more productive than satisfied team members. Think of the implications of that as a leader, not only from a cost perspective but from what's possible in your organization if it's filled with inspired people. An inspired individual can do the work of 2.5 team members because they're going to behave wildly differently than any other type of contributor. This productivity is driven by some of the most important effects of inspiration like energy, excitement, and a sense of purpose. Inspiration has a dramatic impact on how people show up, produce, and engage. They become invested, exceptionally productive, and intensely focused.

Let's take the numbers out of it for a minute. Imagine how an organization of inspired employees would feel— not only inside the organization but beyond it, when engaging with vendors, clients and customers, and the community at large. For an organization focused on solving a challenging social problem like homelessness or a devastating health problem like cancer, imagine how a group of wildly inspired people would tackle that issue and what their potential for solving it might be.

I'm willing to bet that the next question you might have is how to inspire your employees. It's a logical question. But here's the deal: As leaders, it isn't our job to help people be inspired in the moment; it's our job to help them set the stage for inspiration. Many of us know the old adage that you can lead a horse to water but you can't make them drink, or as one of my clients likes to point out, you can't push 'em in either. Our job as leaders is to lead others to the well of inspiration. We'll talk about specific paths we can take to inspire people in a later section.

Deeper Connection to Cause

Inspiration in the work context is often tied to shared values and goals. That's why it's so important to screen for this fit between the potential employee and the culture and mission of the organization when hiring.

I'll go back to what I said earlier about inspiration being optional. Assuring alignment between every employee and your mission/vision/values isn't critical. You can function beautifully with satisfied and even engaged employees. But when our employees do have that deep connection to the cause, sparks fly.

Let's return to you, the leader. Inspired leaders transform:

» their employees

» their companies

» their communities

» themselves

We've made a case for why inspiration deserves a seat at the table (preferably next to caffeine and courage). Now it's time to get specific, because not all sparks are the same. In the next chapter, we'll draw a clear line between "inspired by" (the lift) and "inspired to" (the leap), and why knowing the difference is key to turning possibility into progress.

3

INSPIRED BY VS. INSPIRED TO

To know how to inspire others, and how to put inspiration to work in your own life, you need to understand and navigate the distinction between the two types of inspiration: "inspired by" and "inspired to."

When you are *inspired by* something, you feel inspired but aren't drawn to act. When you are *inspired to*, you're compelled to action. The former allows for some reflection, positive feelings, and perhaps a small shift in thinking, while the latter drives momentum and activity.

Nature provides abundant *inspired by* moments. You may be out camping and wake up to a gorgeous, rosy-cheeked sunrise, and as you're watching the pink spread across the sky, you feel a corresponding openness of inspiration spreading across your chest. Are you inspired? Absolutely. Are you inspired to take action? Perhaps. Maybe you make a promise to yourself to watch more sunrises or to wake up earlier to get a better start to your day. Maybe the sunrise inspires you to take up photography again or to spend more time in nature. But for many of us, we feel inspiration, and then we carefully place the memory into our catalog of experiences as something that was delightful or joyful but not necessarily anything that moved us closer to a dream or goal.

Inspired to is exactly as it sounds: a flash of inspiration compels you to act. Let's say that you've always dreamed of opening a bakery. You came out of undergrad, worked for a bakery, ended up in law school, and now you find yourself a successful, highly paid, completely burned-out attorney. While you spend what little free time you have working on new recipes or designing the new logo for your bakery-to-be, your practical mind convinces you that your life right now is . . . fine. You're making a great living, you're well-respected at your firm and in your field, and the work is challenging but rewarding. And even with all of that being true, you still crave the chance to do something different. To be someone different. One morning you read the story of a local woman who lives a few towns over, also an attorney, who has a green thumb and a passion for plants, left the legal profession and started a plant nursery that's now thriving. You're electrified by the story. It feels like a sign from the universe giving you the permission you weren't able to give yourself previously to start looking into the next steps it would take for you to open that bakery.

When we're inspired by the stories of other people, we often think, "If they can do it, I can do it too."

A quick note about semantics here. While we say we're *inspired by* a person, in most cases what's activated is *inspired to*.

The people who inspire us provide a vision of what's possible. Not only does it feel possible, but in moments of inspiration, it also feels attainable. We see ourselves in those inspiring figures: the parent who published their first children's book after their kids grew up, the office administrator who launched a cleaning service empire, the attorney who had the midlife career pivot to follow their passion. That person we admire may not be who we are now, but they show us who we could be. And we realize it's possible. Inspiration is witnessing someone (including yourself) overcoming fear, uncertainty, and doubt.

Of course we don't all find inspiration in the same sources. What determines which stories or examples spur us to act? Our values and goals.

The newspaper article about the attorney who opened the plant store? For the rest of us who read it, we may only be inspired to go buy yet another houseplant. But for that attorney with similar goals to start a new business based on her passion, the article is the "sign" she needed to take the next step to bring her closer to her dreams.

The story of Roger Bannister is another example of the difference between *inspired by* vs. *inspired to.* Bannister was the first man to break the four-minute mile in competition. It happened in 1954, but the story really starts eight years earlier, when a lanky seventeen-year-old Oxford student decided to give running a go. He wasn't a prodigy grinding out laps from childhood. He trained lightly, casually, even. And yet, a year later, he clocked a 4:26 mile. The 1948 Olympics came and went, and while Bannister was invited to compete, he declined. He knew he wasn't ready, but watching those games lit a fire in him. He wasn't just *inspired by* the Olympians—he was *inspired to* become one of them. So he made a decision: He'd train for the 1952 Games, and he'd go for gold.

Bannister ramped up his training but skipped most races in 1951 to conserve his energy for the 1,500-meter race at the Olympics. When the Olympics rolled around in Helsinki, the format changed. Runners now had to run two heats instead of one, and it threw him off. He made it to the final heat but ran out of gas, finishing seventh. The result was certainly not what he'd dreamed of.

Disappointed, he almost quit. But after some soul-searching (and probably a few long runs), he set a new goal: run a mile in less than four minutes. At the time, it was considered physically impossible—like trying to lasso the wind.

By 1953, he'd shaved his time down to 4:03.6. The problem was that both Wes Santee from the US and John Landy from Australia were aiming for the same thing. The clock was ticking.

In May 1954, at a meet between Oxford and the British Amateur Athletic Association of England, Bannister lined up. More than three thousand people packed the stands. The BBC broadcast the race live. And at precisely 6:03:59.4 p.m., Roger Bannister did what no human had done before in recorded history: he ran a mile in 3:59.4. A number that shattered not just a record but a mental barrier.

People still talk about this accomplishment. What's most compelling isn't just *what* he did, it's *why*. As Bannister said, "Even then people were talking about whether it would ever be possible for someone to run a mile in 4 minutes. . . . There was no logic in my mind that if you can run a mile in 4 minutes, 1.25, you can't run it in 3:59. . . . I knew enough medicine and physiology to know it wasn't a physical barrier, but I think it had become a psychological barrier." The moment he stopped chasing other people's medals and started chasing his own impossible, everything changed. Bannister wasn't just inspired by watching greatness. He was inspired to *become* it.

Here we get to the difference between *inspired by* and *inspired to*. How many of us are interested in running a sub-four-minute mile? My guess would be not many. We can be wowed by his achievement and still shovel another spoonful of ice cream in our mouths while we binge watch *The Sopranos* for the fourth time.

But if you have a fitness goal to run a half marathon, to drop your mile time, or set a new, ambitious personal best, maybe Bannister inspires you to train harder or push the limits of what you think your body is capable of. For those pursuing different goals, such as learning a new language or mastering an instrument, his story may be less inspiring.

If we value innovation in science or technology, the stories of Thomas Edison or Leonardo da Vinci may resonate with us. Entrepreneurs who want to start a business may take action after reading the stories of Howard Schultz or Vera Wang. But we shouldn't confuse admiration with inspiration. You can admire and respect someone like Jane Goodall, but without a shared value or goal, her story will not inspire you to act.

Fame and fortune aren't necessary for us to be inspired by other people. We can look to Mother Teresa or Martin Luther King Jr., to Greta Thunberg or Jane Goodall, to leaders in our local communities or mentors at work.

One more point about *inspired by* vs. *inspired to* and the connection between the two types of inspiration. *Inspired by* can often precede *inspired to* because it creates a sense of openness.

Inspiration, in part, is about broadening our horizons and giving us perspective. The often-humbling influence of nature, its ability to be awe-inspiring and remind us of a bigger world and things greater than ourselves, gives us the same perspective we look for when we achieve inspiration.

Nature also can set the stage for reframing (which we'll explore in later chapters) because we no longer see ourselves as the biggest or most important thing in our lives.

Inspired by takes us outside of ourselves and puts our attention on something not in our own bodies.

Not all inspiration is created equal. "Inspired by" might stir the soul, but "inspired to" moves the feet. While one gives you a feeling, the other gives you a fire.

But what is that fire, exactly? Where does it come from? Why does one story hit us like lightning while another passes through unnoticed? What's happening in our minds and bodies when we feel that spark—and how do we bottle it, channel it, or even better, create the conditions for it to strike again? To move from inspiration to action, we need to understand the anatomy of inspiration itself. It's time to pop the hood and see how it all works

4

HOW DOES INSPIRATION WORK?

Where do these fleeting moments of inspiration come from? How do we harness their magic? Can we make their magic repeatable?

Let's go back to the psychologists Thrash and Elliot, who laid the groundwork for the study of inspiration. We know, based on their definition, that inspiration is spontaneous, meaning that it happens suddenly, without planning or force. It's your favorite aunt who drops in without notice, just so she can have a coffee with you before she flies off to Paris. It's the double-rainbow that appears just after a spring rain shower, so lovely and vibrant you can't help but smile. It's the sight of a dolphin suddenly jumping out of the water just off the shore. When we apply this spontaneity to real life, inspiration shows up. Inspiration is fleeting by nature. It's the firefly of emotions, appearing suddenly in the darkness to light up our hearts and minds.

The joy of these sudden sparks of inspiration can also be balanced with frustration— especially for those of us who are type A—in that they can't be forced. We can't snap our fingers and conjure up those favorite aunt-rainbow-dolphin moments. Nor is there a recipe that we can methodically follow to ensure that inspiration appears.

So when we want inspiration to show up for us, how do we do it? What's the best way to shine the equivalent of the bat signal into the sky to alert inspiration that we need it?

Just like lightning doesn't strike in a cloudless sky, inspiration emerges most readily when certain mental states align. These ideal conditions create the perfect environment for those sudden flashes of insight. Three key states are particularly important:

1. Spaciousness. This refers to both physical and mental room to breathe, creating an open environment that allows us to be present.

2. Stillness. Once we have spaciousness, we can quiet the mental chatter and eliminate distractions, allowing our minds to settle into the calm receptivity where inspiration can enter stage right.

3. Self-forgetfulness. This is a state of being where we shift our attention away from ourselves and our internal pre-occupations, turning the spotlight outward to others or the world around us. We are no longer the focus of our thoughts.

In the next section we'll talk in greater detail about each of these states of being and also offer ways to achieve them.

The feeling of inspiration requires balance between structure and freedom: the structure required to create the space, and the freedom within the space to feel a sense of inspiration. While we may feel the bolt of inspiration once or twice in our lives, with work we can create the conditions that can help to call inspiration into our lives.

You need discipline to "set the stage" for inspiration to appear, but within that structured space, inspiration requires a looseness and a flow. Think of it like building a garden. The discipline is similar to constructing a well-built fence around the space—the boards are the same height and width and are evenly spaced and carefully painted. There's a very distinct structure, or even a discipline, to that fence. Once we step inside that fence, every-thing changes, with trees and flowers, grasses and ferns. While there's a subtle order, the garden has a wild beauty to it and also a sense of calmness and peace. You sit on a bench listening to the wind blowing through the leaves, watching birds flit back and forth, breathing in the delicate hint of a rose or the heady scent of jasmine. In this receptive state, inspiration could spark at any moment.

I realize I'm asking a lot here. But these two seemingly incongruous concepts of holding something lightly while also enforcing discipline are the keys to experiencing inspiration on a regular basis.

Before we go deeper into the world of inspiration, there's one more traveler we need to meet: motivation. Inspiration and motivation are often mistaken for each other—like twins who dress alike but lead very different lives.

Inspiration may light the fire, but motivation keeps it burning. They are not the same—not in how they move us nor what they ask of us. To understand one, we have to see the other clearly. The next chapter looks closely at motivation—the rhythm beneath the spark.

5

MOTIVATION VS. INSPIRATION

Now we swing the spotlight to motivation. If inspiration is the big idea scribbled on a napkin at 2:00 a.m., motivation is setting the alarm and getting your butt out of bed the next morning to start the work to bring that idea to life. This makes sense. The Latin root of motivation is *movere*, which means to move or to drive to.

Understanding the difference between inspiration and motivation isn't just academic. It has real implications not only for how we lead but also for how we create and sustain progress. Research shows that motivation is often about goal pursuit: it is structured and reward-based, and it can be cultivated through systems, accountability, and next steps. When we create habits and drive change through small actions, motivation is in charge.

Inspiration is more spontaneous and expansive. It taps into vision, values, and identity. When we confuse these two states, we can be left feeling stuck, frustrated, and inadequate. If we expect ourselves to feel inspired before we take action, we may never start. On the flip side, if we rely solely on motivation to grind through without reconnecting to a sense of meaning or possibility, we burn out.

At work, when leaders treat inspiration and motivation interchangeably, we risk misapplying our influence. A team that's burned out doesn't need another deadline; they need a reason to believe again. And an inspired team may simply need more clarity or direction to turn a spark into actual progress toward a goal.

Let's begin with what we think we know: Motivation is commonly defined as the reason someone acts or behaves in a particular way. It's the internal "why" behind doing whatever it is we're doing, whether it's making the call, lacing the shoes, or finishing the spreadsheet. Motivation is forward-focused. It's purposeful, linear, and measurable.

Motivation is the heartbeat of progress, in its steady, deliberate, and forward movement. It lives in the mundane.

Think of it as a mental GPS. While inspiration gives us that split-second, gorgeous view from the top of a mountain of what life could be like before dropping us back into our day-to-day lives, motivation charts the return path to the top, highlights the turns, and gives us the next step. It is rooted in logic, effort, and momentum.

Motivation is practical, step-by-step movement toward something that matters. Inspiration, aside from being more of a feeling than a thought, is exponential, expansive, and intuitive. Inspiration is far less linear. While motivation marches at a steady pace, inspiration leaps, meanders, and sometimes disappears entirely until we're ready to follow it again.

These aren't the only ways that inspiration and motivation differ. Let's cover some of the primary differences between the two to develop an even better understanding.

Conscious and Willed vs. Spontaneous and Unwilled

Motivation is conscious and willed, and inspiration, by definition, is spontaneous and unwilled. For both motivation and inspiration, we can think of the movie *Field of Dreams*. We need to mow the field, put in the bases, add the seats and the dugouts for either state of being to show up. For motivation, the saying "If you build it, they will come" usually applies. If you follow the correct steps, motivation steps up.

Inspiration is more magical and unpredictable. Spaciousness, stillness, and self-forgetfulness might produce a state of inspiration, but there's no guarantee. You still need to build the field, and some nights inspiration steps out of the cornfield like Shoeless Joe Jackson, but some nights it doesn't.

Head vs. Heart

Inspiration is more creative, less practical, and generally, more heart-based than motivation. What does this mean? We lean more heavily into emotion, intuition, and "gut feeling" when inspiration shows up. Part of this is because inspiration, by nature, is evoked and unwilled. Remember our favorite aunt blowing in for a visit without notice? Conversely, motivation is the definition of *will*. Motivation is your grandma who gives you the same set of socks every year because they're practical, dependable, and useful.

Because inspiration is more heart over head, it can sneak past the logical hurdles our brain supplies, like all the reasons why we can't or shouldn't do something. "I can't because I don't have the knowledge, experience, or street cred to take the next step." "We shouldn't because our current revenue projections just don't support hiring that director of operations we know the organization needs in order to ensure our growth."

Inspiration clears these hurdles with ease. If we follow our heart, we can figure it out. Inspiration shows us what's possible by lifting us above the obstacles, while motivation shows us what's practical by keeping our feet firmly planted among the constraints.

Positive vs. Mixed Emotions

While motivation is often driven by reason, we can also be motivated by emotions, both positive and negative. We can choose to achieve a goal either out of passion or fear. Consider getting in better shape. You might be motivated by positive emotions: Inspired by a friend who transformed her health, you envision yourself fitting into those jeans again or having more energy throughout the day.

On the other hand, you might be motivated by fear: Terrified of looking bad next to your fit cousins at your niece's wedding, you imagine being the subject of family gossip. The fear of humiliation and embarrassment is strong enough that you also lace up your running shoes—not to embrace the benefits of a healthy version of you but to run from the fear of judgment.

While motivation can be fueled by either positive or negative emotion, inspiration is always powered by love, by generosity, by hope. Inspiration arrives when your inner Judge quiets down (a more detailed discussion about the Judge happens later in this book). There is no whisper of should or must, and no mental gavel-pounding with the reasons that you can't succeed. It's like a giant vacuum comes along and sucks every ounce of fear out of our bodies. We are not shamed or embarrassed into inspiration. We are pulled by hope or curiosity or purpose.

Our bodies feel different too. Inspiration feels open, light, and expansive. Motivation can feel good, too, but it can also feel grippy or tight. Because motivation relies on logic, we tend to get tangled in reasoning and the need to control outcomes. Inspiration invites us to let go, and in that release, we find freedom and often the insights we've been seeking.

Internal vs. External Connection

Have you ever heard the expression "digging deep"? We're taught to dig deep when the going gets tough, when we need to lower our heads and get through something difficult. It could be muscling through a challenging workout or navigating a painful divorce. It could be a time of very tight cash flow in our business where we're unsure of how we're going to make payroll, or maybe the anxiety and stress of navigating a project or relationship gone sideways. Regardless of the situation, digging deep implies that we go within. We dig deeper within ourselves to find the desire to take the next step and to pull from the knowledge and wisdom we've gained from past experiences to move forward.

Motivation results from focusing inward, revving up our internal drive, gathering our strength and our will power, and using all that momentum to create action.

Inspiration is the opposite. Setting the stage for inspiration relies on three specific states of being, one of which is forgetting the self.

Inspiration swings that giant spotlight from ourselves and our own interior monologue out to another character on stage or to another element in the set.

When we feel inspired, we look to the outside world, to community, to others to help us move forward. We might connect with the friend who was able to get in shape, with the community of musicians who love bluegrass as much as we do, with the fellow CEO and business owners who uniquely understand the challenges we face in our roles. Inspiration comes from a sense of connection with something larger than ourselves.

Strategy/Big Picture vs. Tactics

When we swing that spotlight outside ourselves to beckon in inspiration, we broaden what we illuminate. And when inspiration hits, we also climb up. Our spotlight changes into a searchlight. The perspective we gain in flashes of inspiration are "big picture" moments. We can clearly see a future version of ourselves, a solution, a path forward. It's the view from the mountaintop or the airplane.

If inspiration is about elevation and perspective, motivation is more terrestrial; it's the view from the ground, the "street view" instead of the "satellite view," and it leads us to take the next step or the next few steps.

While we have this larger and more complete view courtesy of inspiration, the details can be hazy. How clearly can we see a coastline when we're flying at thirty thousand feet? We can see where land meets ocean and the sweep of the bays, but we can't see the waves breaking on the shore or the seashells scattered across the sand. Inspiration is the vision, the idea, the outline. Motivation is the markers we use to fill it in. We color in one piece at a time until we're able to complete the entire picture.

We build strategy and vision with inspiration; we build game plans and tactics with motivation.

Purpose vs. Necessity

We may be motivated to do things that are not necessarily tied to our greater purpose. I can be motivated to take the trash out so that the kitchen doesn't start to smell. That (thankfully) has little to do with my greater purpose in life. I can be motivated to take action to avoid punishment, to fit in, to receive monetary awards, to succeed at work. Sometimes the things we're motivated to do cross over with inspiration—especially if they're tied to the internal fire that inspiration ignited.

While inspiration links with meaning, purpose, and values, motivation often comes from necessity or sometimes from an anticipated reward (like not having the house smell like day-old salmon).

In a work setting, an employee who is deeply passionate about creating a sustainable, eco-friendly product line for their company might be inspired by the vision of a better future for the planet. Their drive to innovate grows from a sense of purpose.

Another employee might put in long hours to finish a major project by the deadline. While they take pride in quality work, they are focused on avoiding the consequences of missing a deadline, disappointing their boss, or receiving disciplinary action. Their actions are driven more by obligation than a passion for the work.

Shifts in Beliefs vs. Actions

Stephen Covey's "Be-Do-Have" framework from his book *The 7 Habits of Highly Effective People* highlights the importance of aligning your identity with your actions, which in turn impacts your outcomes. In short, your being will influence what you are doing (or not doing), and those actions dictate what you have.

Inspiration and motivation impact this framework in different places.

Motivation impacts the "Doing" part of the framework. It drives short-term behavioral changes that may affect results temporarily.

Inspiration impacts the "Being" part of the framework. It shifts who you are being, which creates deeper, more lasting changes in both behavior and results.

Let's say a project manager is struggling to advance in her career. She's been in the same role for five years, consistently delivering projects both on time and under budget, yet she gets passed over for promotions. She's trying to figure out what's gone wrong, so she begins by looking at her activities.

She notices that in team meetings, she rarely speaks up unless asked a direct question. She also realizes that while she's been taking detailed notes and executing flawlessly, she's not contributing strategic insights or challenging processes that could be improved.

If she were to use motivation in this scenario, she'd force herself to speak up more in meetings and volunteer for more high-visibility projects. She'd schedule one-on-ones with senior leaders and ask more strategic questions during planning sessions. These shifts in actions could certainly lead to a change in results—more recognition, more visibility, and a higher likelihood of promotion.

But they may not.

Motivation tackles the Doing state, but inspiration tackles the Being state. The question is not only what she is doing or not doing in those meetings, but why?

Let's say she grew up in a household where her voice was not welcome and questioning authority was discouraged. She learned early on that the safest path was to keep her head down and do excellent work quietly. Now, despite her expertise and track record, she believes she's not "leadership material." She believes real leaders are charismatic speakers born to command a room.

This belief bleeds into everything, whether it's her body language during meetings, her reluctance to share her ideas, or her tendency to defer to others even when she has a better solution. As a result, leadership sees her more as a reliable executor than a strategic thinker, and her potential goes unrecognized.

In an inspired state, she identifies who she wants to be: a confident strategic leader who brings valuable perspectives to drive better outcomes. By addressing the root, her Being state, she creates sustainable progress toward the leadership role she deserves.

Inspiration tackles the source, while motivation often tackles the symptoms.

When we compare inspiration and motivation, motivation might look a little dimmer, far less fun, and maybe even like the uptight older brother you never wanted. In a recent workshop, after we outlined the differences between inspiration and motivation and people kept bashing motivation, someone raised their hand and said, "I think motivation is getting a bad rap here." And it's true. It was. So while the two are different, they're both wonderful and needed in their own ways.

Now we know that inspiration and motivation are distinct, each with its own rhythm and role. But they don't show up in their own neat little compartments in a bento box. They overlap, inform, and energize each other in ways that are far from linear. The spark flares, the grind begins, the fire dies, the vision returns. We ebb and flow between them constantly. The next questions are how they work together and when we should rely more heavily on one or the other.

6

THE WONDER TWINS AT WORK

Motivation is inspiration's best friend, its work spouse, its partner in crime. The ying to its yang. They're like the Wonder Twins from the late '70s cartoon *The All-New Super Friends Hour*. The twins, Zan and Jayna, were an extraterrestrial brother and sister who had the power to change shape. While the twins could fight crime and bad guys on their own, they could only activate their superpowers when they were together. "Wonder Twins—activate!" When those superpowers kicked in, that's when the real ass-kicking happened.

Inspiration and motivation are kind of like the Wonder Twins. Can they work on their own? Sure. But they are much better in tandem. Between those trips to the mountaintop of inspiration, when we're slogging through the undergrowth on our way up through the elevation, motivation steps in. It's the fuel that drives us to succeed and to climb the mountain. We need a balanced mix of motivation and inspiration to keep ourselves and our teams on the path to our dreams.

Life rarely gives us the luxury of one pure state at a time. We often find ourselves inspired *and* stuck. Motivated *and* numb. In these moments, it helps to understand how they support each other. One opens us up to possibility, and the other drives us toward action. When they show up together, the path seems clearer, even if it's still difficult.

Let's look at how motivation and inspiration play out in leadership. When do we inspire our employees and when do we motivate them? Ideally, we'll use both inspiration and motivation, but there is a time and a place for each.

Before we can effectively motivate or inspire employees, we need to hire the right people. When employees share our goals and values, they're far more likely to move from passive inspiration to inspired action. Misaligned employees will never embrace the company's vision, no matter how motivational our efforts.

Employees may find meaning and alignment in different ways. Some are drawn to serving specific populations—children, military veterans, or marginalized communities. Others are passionate about creating products that improve vehicle safety or water conditions for fish farms. Many join an organization for its values, whether that's sustainability, innovation, or patriotism. Still others are attracted by the leadership itself.

When people gather with a shared purpose, something magical happens. When they are rallying around the same battle cry and believe in the organization's mission and vision, you can galvanize those who see themselves as part of the collective.

This is why finding and hiring employees who share your company's values is important. Build this into your hiring practices through personality assessment, behavioral interviewing questions, or both. After all, that African proverb rings true: "If you want to go fast, go alone. If you want to go far, go together." It's more powerful when everyone is headed to the same destination.

Let's circle back to inspiration and motivation within organizations. Inspiration is about sharing a vision, a view from the mountaintop for the company, department, team, or whatever group is moving in the same direction. We show people not only where we are now but where we're going and what it will look like when we arrive. The clear blue sky, the hawks drifting on the breeze, the sparkling sea beyond. Here's the key: We paint that picture so carefully and with such detail that people can truly see where the organization is headed and what it will look and feel like when those goals are achieved. It's harder to inspire people when they're operating in the dark, unsure of the end goal or how their work or role contributes to it. An inspirational vision builds on the shared values and goals of the entire community.

One of the best ways to create and convey this compelling vision is through the five components of an inspirational narrative, which we'll explore in part 3. Story is an excellent tool for sharing a vision or an end state. If you're ready to craft an inspirational narrative, feel free to flip to that section—you can always return here.

Inspiring an individual looks different than inspiring an entire organization. We're still giving that employee a vision of the mountaintop, but this time we're envisioning that individual at the peak. The employee is the hero.

Most employees show up to work wanting to do a good job. They want to learn, grow, and excel in their roles. Some hope to move up in the organization and others don't, but regardless of their ambition, most try to do their best. But they sometimes struggle to see their own progress and capabilities.

In my work as an executive coach, I see doubt everywhere. Imposter syndrome, that nagging belief that you're not as capable as others think you are, even when your results and your track record prove otherwise. And fear—of failure, rejection, not being good enough, not belonging. While we can't eliminate these fears for our people, we can help.

When inspiring a team member, our job is to reflect back to them the highest version of themselves. We share all that bottled-up, untapped potential we see in them. We shine a light on the budding skillset we know they can master. We recognize their progress toward goals. We share how we witnessed them overcoming obstacles, learning from mistakes, or dusting themselves off after failure and getting right back on their feet. We discuss next steps in their careers and lives, their future goals and dreams.

Yes, we provide hope and encouragement, but more important, we show them their potential. We show them what they could become and how their aspirations are within reach. We hold up a mirror that reveals what they're capable of and what's possible.

Leadership isn't all sunshine and rainbows. Tough conversations and accountability go along with all of this, but sometimes as leaders we forget our role as the peddlers of hope and possibility. We may become mired in our own day-to-day, the looming goals, the bank covenants, the customer who hasn't paid, the squabbling between departments. We are so focused on the doing, the achieving, the completing, that we forget about the inspiring part.

That's normal.

We've all worked for less-than-inspiring leaders, and we know how that feels. We can feel unappreciated, confused, stuck, or de-motivated. Hopefully you've also had the opportunity to work for wonderfully inspiring leaders. Having had that experience, you can understand the importance of inspiring people.

Touched by inspiration, our people will be more open, more curious, and more creative. They'll work smarter and not harder. Their curiosity will more quickly lead to collaboration instead of finger-pointing, to communication instead of isolation. The teams will all row in the same direction because they'll know which direction is the right one and how their role contributes to the entire team reaching the destination.

Inspiration changes the way we process information, often shifting perceptions and beliefs. Motivation may shift thoughts, but more often, it will shift action. If we want to make a longer-term or deeper shift in someone's perception, it's better to inspire than to motivate.

Let's use an example of a sales team and a suite of products. InnovateX Solutions launched a new product meant to upgrade their current product offering. Despite marketing, training, and new incentives, the sales team continues to sell tons of product A but very little of the new product B. The products are similarly priced, product B has more features, and leadership has been clear about shifting focus to product B.

Our first step is determining if the sales team lacks drive or passion: motivation or inspiration.

When leadership talks to the sales reps, they learn that customers like product A and rarely complain about it. But when they sell product B, despite being newer and having more features, they receive far more questions and complaints. As a result, they believe in product A but lack confidence in product B.

What the leadership team is actually seeing is that the sales reps' perceptions and beliefs about the products drive their emotions and confidence. Those confidence levels impact their actions. They are far more likely to mention and sell product A. They're more hesitant about presenting the new offer. Their tone of voice may be different, they may hesitate while answering questions, or they stumble over their words. This ties directly to results—far greater sales of product A than product B.

The leadership team can shift results two ways. If they choose to motivate the team to sell more of product B, all they need to do is adjust the commission plan. Pay more to sell product B to shift activity levels (especially for money-motivated reps). But this doesn't address the sales reps' belief that product B is inferior. We may see temporary gains without changing the entire sales team's behavior.

If we choose to inspire the team, we'll shift their beliefs, which will have a much longer-lasting and deeper impact.

To shift beliefs, we must understand how they formed. Why do sales reps think product B is a dud? Customer feedback seems damning, but digging deeper reveals that sales reps don't understand product B's new features. They can't explain them well, so customers get frustrated, too, because they don't understand them either.

With proper training on product B's features, benefits, and functionality, sales reps can educate customers before and after the sale. Complaints decrease, satisfaction improves, and sales reps shift their perceptions based on new customer feedback.

That's one way to shift mindset. The second way? Tell them a story. A story about a fellow sales rep who successfully sold product B to a happy customer shows the sales team it's possible. Remember, inspiration is seeing what's possible, shifting our belief that something is out of reach.

Inspiration makes our belief systems more malleable. Motivation doesn't have nearly the same impact.

There's a time and a place for both. When your team is focused, they're clear on the goal they need to achieve, but they may have run out of a bit of steam, so motivation is the way to go. But if you've got a team that seems to have lost direction, they're not sure where they're headed or why, then inspiration is your best course of action.

In one last example, a colleague was struggling to start a new project. We talked about all the reasons why he was having trouble and identified two core issues: this person's Avoider Saboteur and their fear of rejection. (For more on the Avoider Saboteur, go to www.positiveintelligence.com and take the free assessment to learn more about your saboteurs.)

To help him overcome these blocks, we tried two different approaches to see what would be more effective. First, we had him imagine the positive impacts: the difference his project would make in people's lives, the financial benefits for him, and how it aligned with his purpose.

Second, we had him make a wager with the group. If he didn't complete the project within a few months, he would burn all his beloved college team gear. (Go 'Zags, and as of this moment, I'm happy to report that no Gonzaga gear was burned in this exercise.)

We asked which was more motivating for him, the inspiration of what could be or the motivation driven by a potential negative outcome—the pull or the push?

He said, by far, it was the push.

Yikes.

So what does that mean for inspiration? Does it mean that we should throw away all our carrots and go break off more sticks to use on ourselves and on our people?

No. Here's why.

My colleague was clear about the mountaintop. He knew his goal and the impact it would have on other people. He knew how it fit into his values and his biggest dreams about what he wanted to accomplish and his desired legacy. All of those things were crystal clear.

He had already had his flash of inspiration that helped him identify the dream.

What he needed now was motivation.

When our goal is identified and we need to move, motivation is the key. The mountaintop can be radiant with sunshine and haloed with clouds, but trying to identify the best path to scale the mountain can be daunting. There are a hundred different ways we could reach the top, a hundred "next steps" we could take. Where do we start? What's the "right" way to do it? What else should we be considering? How do we prepare? Before you know it, even though we're looking at those beautiful purple mountains majesty, we're rooted in place.

Motivation is about movement, whether figurative or literal. It's peeling the soles of our feet off the ground and taking that first step, or the hundredth, or thousandth, in pursuit of our highest selves and our loftiest goals.

Motivation works best just after we've been inspired, when the whisper of our dream still lingers but we're unsure how to proceed. It helps us narrow our scope and define the next step or the next few steps, and it gives us a push to get moving when we're stuck in place.

We use motivation when we are clear on where we're headed but are just having trouble getting there.

Inspiration helps us determine our goal.

So now you've got the tools. You know when to fire up the engine and when to wait for the spark. But what's your current state? Before we continue, let's take a quick quiz to check in on your level of inspiration at work. (No wrong answers. No grade. Just a little self-awareness.)

After that, we'll explore something equally important: how to create the conditions that allow inspiration to return. Although you can't force inspiration to show up, you can learn how to clear space for it. You can learn how to listen. And most often, it shows up in the quiet when we make room for spaciousness, stillness, and self-forgetfulness.

INSPIRATION QUIZ

Curious about your inspiration quotient? Eight quick questions will show you where you stand with inspiration on the job (dive deeper with the personal version at sparkinggreatness.com).

1. **What is the degree of clarity you have on your overall purpose and goals in your organization?**
    a. Crystal clear.
    b. Vision is a little cloudy, but I've got the gist.
    c. It's murky down here—I've got spots of clarity and a lot of confusion.
    d. Pitch-black darkness—I can't see my hand in front of my own face!

2. **Rate your level of understanding of the impact you or your organization is making on the world or on the lives of your customers.**
    a. I can clearly see the positive impact that I have on my organization and that our organization has on the world.
    b. I feel like I'm making a positive impact on our organization, but sometimes I wonder about how we're impacting our clients.
    c. There are glimpses of our impact on our customers, but sometimes I doubt my own impact on my organization.
    d. I'm not clear on how I benefit the organization or the organization is benefitting our clients.

3. **How connected are you to your clients?**
   a. I meet with or speak with our clients on a weekly basis.
   b. I touch base with clients a few times a quarter.
   c. I don't interact with clients directly but get feedback on their experience through other channels.
   d. I'm fairly disconnected from our clients.

4. **When you wake up in the morning and you think about work, you feel:**
   a. Energized and motivated—go go gadget work!
   b. Perfectly fine—even-keel.
   c. Meh.
   d. It's all I can do to crawl to the coffee maker.

5. **The amount of time you feel like you have in your day to sit and ponder things is:**
   a. About an hour a day of uninterrupted time—more if I plan in advance.
   b. Potential to grab fifteen to twenty minutes about once a day.
   c. Maybe ten minutes a few times a week.
   d. Every minute of every day is filled (and I'm exhausted).

6. **Your ability to focus is best described as:**
   a. It's a twelve-lane highway of thoughts in my brain twenty-four hours a day—nothing slows those thoughts down.
   b. I can get short period of focus. Pomodoro method works for me.
   c. I'm able to focus sixty to ninety minutes at a time.
   d. Once I get started on something, I get lost in it—hours can pass without me knowing.

7. **Select the frequency with which you engage with a community (anything from a nonprofit to a cycling club, a religious group, or a professional organization).**
   a. Very frequently
   b. Often
   c. Less frequently
   d. Never

8. **My current level of motivation at work is:**
   a. High—I am ready to jump over buildings.
   b. Medium—I feel motivated to achieve most projects and initiatives.
   c. Medium low—Motivation comes in fits and spurts, far and few between.
   d. Low—It's hard for me to focus, and I feel like I've got so much to do—I'm drowning.

9. **I'd describe my current level of overwhelm as:**
   a. I'm so far below water I don't know which way is up.
   b. I feel pretty overwhelmed at the moment but know that there's an end in sight.
   c. I'm overwhelmed from time to time, but things generally seem manageable.
   d. I feel like things are under control and moving along at a good pace.

10. **The last time I remember feeling inspired was:**
    a. Sometime in the last thirty days.
    b. Within the last six months.
    c. Within the past year.
    d. I honestly can't remember.

How to Calculate Your Score

1. **Answer each question** by choosing the option that best reflects your current experience.

2. **Assign points** to your answers:
   - » A = **4 points**
   - » B = **3 points**
   - » C = **2 points**
   - » D = **1 point**

3. **Add up your points** across all the questions to get your total score.

4. **Use your total score** to find your inspiration profile:
   - » **28–32 points** → *The Visionary Spark:* Your inspiration is burning bright. You're leading with clarity, connection, and purpose—and it shows.
   - » **22–27 points** → *The Engaged Leader:* You're motivated and making a difference, but you may sense there's another level waiting.
   - » **16–21 points** → *The Flickering Flame:* You're feeling some wins, but leadership may feel more like a grind than a calling.
   - » **8–15 points** → *The Dim Light:* Your inspiration tank is low. Life at work may feel heavy or disconnected. The good news? Even a small spark can reignite the flame.

For more reflection prompts and next steps for each inspiration profile, please go to sparkinggreatness.com.

PART 2
CLEARING THE PATH

7

DEALING WITH OVERWHELM AND BURNOUT

In part 1 we explored what inspiration is and why it matters. Now we're getting into the good stuff: creating conditions that make inspiration more likely to show up. Think of this as getting the guest room ready before someone wildly creative and unpredictable arrives (like our favorite Aunt Madge).

My research has led me to identify three states that consistently precede inspiration: spaciousness, stillness, and self-forgetfulness.

However, I know it's much easier to create spaciousness when life isn't pressing in from all sides, when we're not already stretched too thin or emotionally wrung out. But what happens when we are? What if the idea of "creating space" seems impossible?

If inspiration needs space to breathe, then we first must talk about what happens when we can't find any, in those moments when you're too depleted to slow down or step back.

When you're overwhelmed or burned out, spaciousness becomes impossible. So that's where we're headed next—to clear the debris blocking the path to inspiration.

8

THE PERISCOPE EFFECT: NAVIGATING FROM OVERWHELM TO CLARITY

Spaciousness sounds beautiful, but when you're buried under deadlines, decisions, and emotional fatigue, it's hard enough to find the floor, let alone the sky. During the past several years, I've seen more clients in overwhelm or burnout as the world changes at an ever-accelerating pace. They're surrounded by so many projects, tasks, meetings, and must-dos that they struggle to prioritize or make progress on any of the items on their list.

This is exactly where Nicole was, a CEO who runs an outsourced professional services firm. The firm was outgrowing its infancy and needed several changes to reach the next stage of growth. Nicole was simultaneously building a stronger infrastructure, managing loyal but underperforming employees who needed to be moved out, changing product offerings, adding clients who were a better fit for these new product lines, and implementing new company-wide software platforms to help increase efficiency. She was also still doing some direct client work herself. Even with a business partner, most decisions fell to her.

When we'd discuss these issues, she described feeling that, just as she made progress in one area, something else would pull her away. Any progress felt so small or insignificant, it seemed almost not worth doing. She was exhausted and overwhelmed.

Overwhelm has many facets. Think back on your own experience and see if any of these sound familiar:

Overexposed vs. Intentionally Open

When we're overwhelmed, we're usually too open. Too many things fill our bandwidth, making it hard to focus on any one thing. Everything is blurred because there's just so much in terms of to-dos, thoughts, and feelings. We lose control over what we let into our lives.

Reactive vs. Reflective

Overwhelm keeps us too busy reacting to reflect. In survival mode, we don't have the space or energy to be reflective or discerning. We're also unable to zoom out to get a greater perspective or reframe anything that's currently in our mental space. Our executive function, the set of mental skills that help us plan, focus, and manage our actions to reach goals, is limited and so is our curiosity.

Habitual vs. Intentional

When inundated, we cling to what we already know. Even if those habits or patterns aren't healthy or helpful, we default to what is known and comfortable instead of making intentional decisions. Overwhelm crowds out everything else, limiting our openness to new ideas, concepts, or choices.

Frozen or Frantically Busy (Stuck Either Way) vs. Making Progress

Overload can be deceptive. Depending on how overstimulated we are, we can still look incredibly productive. Normally, we're busier but less productive. Deeper overload states bordering on burnout look like a total lack of action or decision. Regardless of what shows up, all decisions feel paralyzing or pressure-filled, and we feel like we're not making meaningful progress in any area.

Isolated vs. Connected

While spaciousness nurtures connection to ourselves and others, overwhelm severs these connections and prevents us from taking action to reconnect. In overwhelm, we withdraw from others because we don't have the capacity to connect. When we carve out even a few minutes of quiet, whether to journal, take a walk, or simply breathe, we create room to notice our own thoughts and emotions. That presence spills outward and makes it easier to listen deeply, show empathy, and engage meaningfully with the people around us.

Self-Absorbed vs. Self-Aware

By self-absorbed, I don't mean selfish. When our nervous system is blown, focusing on anything outside of ourselves can be difficult. This state also limits our self-awareness. When we're blown out, we're less conscious of how we show up and behave.

These aspects of overwhelm matter, especially the last one. While some people recognize when they're overloaded, others can't. Their field of view is so limited, and their self-awareness is so low, that they just feel tired and super busy.

Moving from overwhelm to inspiration isn't impossible, but it's complicated. Why? Recall the state of being most people are in when they have a flash of inspiration: spaciousness, ability to focus and reframe, and curiosity. We often think of inspiration as elevation, as a shooting star in the night sky, or as the shining peak of a mountain.

In comparison, overwhelm feels like scuba diving in the deepest parts of the ocean. The likelihood that you can get someone from several thousand feet below sea level to several thousand feet above in one session isn't great. Nor would you want to try.

Like scuba divers ascending slowly from a deep dive to avoid the bends, people emerging from burnout need gradual decompression. Attempting to extract someone out of overwhelm too quickly often sends them back where they started. The help that's offered can seem like one more thing added to the stack of items on a list.

Common reasons we slide into overwhelm:

» High expectations and demands: These may be imposed by others or ourselves. Unrealistically high standards and an unmanageable workload are among the most common factors for burnout and ongoing stress.

» Feeling unappreciated or undervalued: When our work and efforts go unrecognized, it erodes motivation and increases exhaustion.

» A sense of isolation or lack of understanding: Feeling alone in our struggles, whether because of physical separation or lack of emotional support, increases the risk of overwhelm.

Continuing with the scuba diving metaphor: Overwhelm makes us feel like we're underwater, but we can still see the light shining above. Burnout is when we've hit the ocean floor; there's no light, and we've given up.

Our feelings in overwhelm differ from those of burnout.

OVERWHELM	BURNOUT
Feelings of worry and stress	Very little feeling, lack of engagement, apathy
"If I can just get everything under control . . ."	"There's no way this will ever happen . . ."
Sense of urgency	Complete lack of urgency

The distinction between the overwhelm and burnout is important because we treat them differently. Overwhelm needs more immediate triage and boundary setting, while burnout requires deep, systemic change and often professional support.

I recently worked with Elizabeth, a busy CEO and mom, who had sunk all the way to the bottom of overwhelm and experienced a prolonged and deep sense of burnout.

She had just lost a cherished employee to suicide, navigated difficult family dynamics within her business, and led her company successfully through a pandemic. She was exhausted and beyond overwhelmed for so long that she was completely burned out.

When Elizabeth first experienced burnout, we kept having conversations about her dreams, what she wanted to do next, and what she saw for herself. However, she was frustrated when she was unable to articulate much along these lines. Because burnout leaves us in this inky darkness, it's hard to see the light at the end of any tunnel. The depression and apathy we feel for almost everything becomes almost as challenging as the burnout itself.

This is one reason it's so hard to inspire someone who feels burned out. One precursor for inspiration is a sense of connection. When we're in deep burnout, our ability to feel joy or connection is severely limited. We're mostly feeling a bone-deep exhaustion, completely powerless, and a desire to walk away from it all.

One last vivid image to compare overwhelm and burnout: Overwhelm is carrying ten different grocery bags while trying to balance car keys, a coffee, and a dog leash and we're lurching around on the sidewalk. Burnout is when we've been carrying all of those things for so long that we face-plant on the cement.

So now that you're figuratively laying on the sidewalk, how do you get up off your face?

The next several chapters present strategies to create a periscope to guide you from the depths of overwhelm and burnout back up to the surface. I'll share some of the strategies that Nicole and Elizabeth used to invite inspiration into their lives again.

Remember the oxygen mask analogy? We need to care for ourselves in order to care for others. Each chapter will provide specifics about implementing these practices in your own life, and some also include ways in which you can bring these practices to your organization.

At the end of each chapter in the next few sections, you'll find short, practical exercises designed to help you bring the ideas off the page and into your life. Each one has two parts: one for your own reflection and growth, and one to apply with your team. Use them as prompts, conversation starters, or checkpoints to turn inspiration into action. And remember, these aren't tests. Give yourself grace as you move through them. The goal is progress, not perfection.

EXERCISES

For You: Predicting Your Overwhelm

1. **Overwhelm Patterns:** Map your personal and professional overwhelm triggers. When do they typically occur? (Examples could be holidays, work cycles, life transitions.) What early warning signs can you identify before you're fully underwater?

2. **Your Overwhelm Signature:** What does overwhelm look like specifically for you? More TV, less exercise? More scrolling, less listening? Create a personal "overwhelm inventory" of the behaviors, thoughts, and physical sensations that signal you're moving toward overwhelm.

For Your Team: Creating Overwhelm Awareness

1. **Organizational Overwhelm Audit:** Assess your team's overwhelm patterns. What systemic factors (unclear priorities, understaffing, broken processes, etc.) contribute to overwhelm in your organization? When does your team collectively struggle most?

2. **Leadership Alignment Check:** Examine the gap between what you say and what you model. Where might your actions be contributing to team overwhelm despite good intentions? How can you better align your leadership behavior with the spaciousness you want to create?

9

THE BIG FOUR: BUILDING YOUR RECOVERY FOUNDATION

When we're in burnout or feeling overwhelmed, our first task is to recognize and then own it. I often see clients in denial about their overwhelm. "I've got it covered," they tell me. While I'm sure that's the case in their minds, it doesn't mean they're not actually overwhelmed.

The last chapter helped identify if we're in overwhelm or burnout, and assuming that's true, where do we start to remedy the situation?

If you're familiar with Maslow's hierarchy of needs, we start with the very bottom layer of the pyramid: physiological needs. It's the best place to begin if you want to make an immediate impact on overwhelm.

Maslow's Hierarchy of Needs

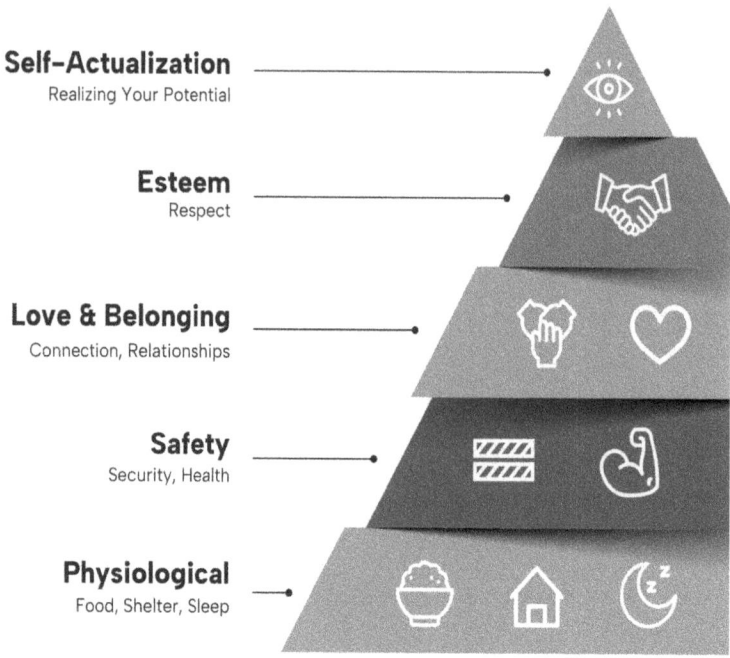

Self–Actualization
Realizing Your Potential

Esteem
Respect

Love & Belonging
Connection, Relationships

Safety
Security, Health

Physiological
Food, Shelter, Sleep

I see clients bypassing these needs on a regular basis but even more so when they're overloaded.

Assuming that food, shelter, and warmth are taken care of, let's address what I call "the Big Four" one at a time.

Nutrition: When your body is undernourished, your brain reads that as danger. Balanced meals are as much about energy as they are about stability. When we feel overwhelmed, we may grab what's fastest, and many of those choices can spike and crash our blood sugar, which only amplifies the chaos. I am a sucker for hot, salty fries or soft serve, and I notice how much more frequently I eat them when I feel like I'm buried. Junk food does not help my ability to access my wisdom or slim my waistline. We run into similar issues when we skip meals or overeat.

Hydration: Even mild dehydration can mimic anxiety and make you feel foggy, fatigued, or irritable. What cues does your body give when you're dehydrated? You could start cramping, feel fatigued, or get a headache at the base of your skull. If you're feeling overwhelmed, check your water bottle. Let's hope it doesn't have dust gathering on it. Conversely, you may be patting yourself on the back for all the liquid you've consumed because you're on your fourth cup of coffee for the day, and although I love that for you in all your caffeinated brilliance, it's not the same as four glasses of water (yes, I know it has water in it; still not the same).

Sleep: Sleep is the foundation your brain relies on. Without enough rest, it's hard to regulate your emotions, prioritize tasks, or make decisions, all of which are needed for you to dig out of overwhelm. The Mayo Clinic recommends that adults get at least seven hours of sleep per night. It's okay to short yourself every now and again, but make an effort for a consistent seven hours per night. Some clients tell me they don't need more than six hours a night. Do I buy that? Not really. Inadequate sleep contributes to overwhelm and burnout. Period.

Breath: We don't often pay attention to our breath outside of meditation or yoga sessions. When you're in overwhelm, your breath gets shallow and fast. It signals your nervous system that you're in danger, and all of a sudden you've got cortisol and adrenaline, your body's stress hormone and "fight-or-flight" hormone, dumping into your body. Those hormones don't help. It may sound silly, but paying attention to how and when you're breathing can make an immediate impact on overwhelm.

Physical needs affect our nervous system and our fight-or-flight systems. As you can imagine, being in fight-or-flight mode limits our ability to feel a sense of spaciousness. Addressing gaps in our basic needs increases our ability to feel that sense of openness.

By attending to these basic needs, you send your nervous system the signal that you're all right. This isn't just getting out of survival mode and instead moving closer to the surface out of overwhelm; it's the beginning of spaciousness.

Just like Andy Dufrane didn't escape from prison in a day in *Shawshank Redemption*, we don't escape burnout quickly either. If you're still stuck in the spiral of too muchness, even after solid sleep and a balanced breakfast for a couple of weeks, we've got more tools in the tool shed. We'll explore the power of movement in the next chapter.

EXERCISES

For You: The Big Four Assessment

1. **Your Body's Report Card:** Over the next three days, track your Big Four without judgment—just awareness. Questions to ask:

   Nutrition: Are you eating enough food for your body throughout the day, or are you skipping meals? Conversely, are you overeating due to stress? Either way, what type of foods and beverages are you choosing to fuel yourself with?

   Hydration: How are your hydration levels? How many ounces of fluid do you drink on a daily basis? How many of those ounces are? How often are you choosing sugary drinks, caffeine, or alcohol?

   Sleep: What does your sleep schedule look like? What time is your head hitting the pillow? How many hours a night? Is it uninterrupted? Do you have trouble falling asleep? How many times are you up in the night? Are you able to get back to sleep?

   Breath: If you were to sit still for a moment and notice your breathing pattern, what do you feel? Are you breathing deeply, or is your breath shallow? Does it reach down into your belly? Are you holding tension in your body? If so, where is it? How can you stretch, drop your shoulders, or move your body to release it?

Note energy levels, mood, and focus alongside your nutrition, hydration, sleep, and breathing patterns. What connections do you notice?

2. **The One-Thing Strategy:** Based on your tracking, choose just ONE of the Big Four to focus on improving for the next week. What's the smallest change you could make that would have the biggest impact on your overwhelm?

For Your Team: Modeling Basic Needs

1. **The Hydration Challenge Plus:** Create a team hydration challenge but expand it beyond water. Track team energy and meeting effectiveness during the challenge week. The winner gets to choose the office playlist, select the next team lunch spot, or receive a wellness-focused prize (massage gift card, premium water bottle, etc.).

2. **Meeting Wellness Audit:** Examine your meeting culture through a basic needs lens. Are you scheduling back-to-back meetings that prevent bathroom/water breaks? Running through lunch? Scheduling early-morning or late-evening calls that impact sleep? What one meeting practice could you change to better support your team's physiological needs?

10

MOVE A MUSCLE, CHANGE A THOUGHT

As a procrastinator with raging undiagnosed ADHD in high school, I had a tough time studying. It was not uncommon for me to go from focused to overwhelmed while sitting at the kitchen table, staring blankly at notecards with my head in my hands.

When my mom would come into the kitchen to refresh her coffee or empty her ashtray, she could see that not much was getting done. I remember one time while I was studying for my AP History exam and drowning in overwhelm.

My mom put down her coffee mug and ashtray and came over to stand in front of me.

"Get up," she said.

I looked at her like she was crazy.

"Mom, I'm studying."

"No, you're staring off into space with your head in your hands. That doesn't look like studying to me."

"There's just so much—I'm never going to get it all done."

Instead of arguing with me, or consoling me, she challenged me to move.

"Okay. Here's what you're going to do. You're going to get up, put your shoes on, go outside, and run around the house three times. When you're done, you're going to come in, drink a glass of water, and have a snack. After you're finished eating, you and I are going to talk about next steps, and then you can get back to studying."

Despite my eye rolls and exasperated teenage sighs, I did what she told me. And despite my doubt, it worked. Once I came back in from my laps and had my water and snack, she sat me down and helped me create a much more manageable study plan, one piece at a time. You'll notice that she made sure my basic needs were being met in the moment.

After this, her mantra moving forward, whenever she saw me in overwhelm was, "Move a muscle, change a thought."

Now my go-to when I notice symptoms of overwhelm in myself or others is to put on shoes and go for a walk. It doesn't need to be a twenty-mile march— up and down the street or around the block is fine. If the weather outside is lousy, walk around the inside of your home.

Here's the secret: Your body can lead your mind. Any type of movement can interrupt the loop of overwhelm you may be caught in. It shakes loose the mental debris, gets your energy going in a new direction, and gives you a fresh entry point for the challenge your brain may be swirling around.

The change not only in movement but also in scenery is a palate cleanser for our brains.

Once I'm back at the desk or in the room with a client, we work on narrowing our focus. Overwhelm is often caused by too many stimuli, such as a cascade of inputs from email and Slack, from text messages and emails, from co-workers, friends, family. All of these inputs create a to-do list that seems endless, and we feel like there's not nearly enough time to do it all. (Hint: There isn't. Letting go of perfection will help.)

This is on top of app notifications, the news we watch or read, audiobooks, podcasts, listening to the radio, etc. And we wonder why we get so overwhelmed?

We know that taking a break to move a muscle does change a thought and reminds us that we're not stuck. It's an easy pattern interrupt that gives your thoughts space to reassemble more easily.

But clearing your mind works only for so long if the onslaught of inputs continues your way. We need to look at limiting inputs to allow us to focus on what's important.

EXERCISES

For You: Movement as Mental Reset

1. **Your Movement Menu:** Identify three to five different types of movement that work for you in different situations— something for when you're stuck at a desk (e.g., shoulder rolls, desk push-ups), something for when you have five minutes (walk around the building), and something for when you have more time (e.g., neighborhood walk, dance session). Test them this week and note which ones most effectively shift your mental state.

2. **The Overwhelm Circuit Breaker:** When you notice overwhelm building, commit to moving before you try to solve anything. Track for one week: How often did you catch overwhelm early enough to interrupt it with movement? What was the difference in your problem-solving ability after movement versus trying to push through without it?

For Your Team: Energy Management in Real Time

1. **Meeting Movement Protocol:** Establish a team norm for movement breaks during long meetings. Experiment with different approaches: scheduled two-minute movement breaks every thirty minutes, or give everyone permission

to call for a "movement moment" when they notice energy flagging. Track meeting effectiveness and engagement.

1. **The Wilty Flower Intervention:** Train your team to recognize and respond to "wilty flower syndrome" in each other. Create a simple signal system where team members can indicate when they need a mental reset, and practice different group energizers.

2. **Virtual Roller Coaster:** This is one of my favorite foils for "wilty flower syndrome." Have everyone lean back in their chairs with their hands on their chest as though they're holding on to the safety bars of a roller coaster. As you get to the top of the virtual roller coaster, everyone puts their hands in the air as the roller coaster dives down, you sway back and forth (and you, the facilitator, are yelling out directions and generally making a fool of yourself) until the ride "ends." People will be energized, lighter. They may think you're a little nuts, and that's okay too.

11

INFORMATION DIET

In a single hour, you may get five texts, respond to thirty Slack pings, read two news headlines, listen to a podcast about how you're doing life wrong, and see a calendar reminder that you're supposed to bring snacks for basketball practice tonight. Overwhelm isn't about just what's inside of us. It's created by what we choose to let in.

Remember our overwhelm vs. burnout analogy and our figurative bags of groceries? This chapter is about exploring boundaries, editing what gets access to your brain, and creating enough quiet in your mind for spaciousness by putting down some of those bags.

Part of the reason it can be hard to get out of overwhelm and burnout is that not only do we continue to try and balance all of the grocery bags with everything else in our lives, we keep collecting even more.

Our first step is to stop. We don't need more; we need less. Instead of spreading our energy and our time over so many people, places, and things, what if we start pulling some of that time and energy back into ourselves?

When we go from overwhelm to burnout, it's often the multitude of inputs that make us finally keel over. Limiting our inputs and focusing on just a few things is a good first step. It allows us to begin to build energy and focus, because by the time we get to burnout, we're out of both.

Where to start? It begins by creating a sense of control that makes it possible to consider spaciousness.

One of those bags that you'll want to put down first is full of screens. Not only the number of screens you interact with between cell phones, tablets, laptops, and TVs but also how you behave with each of them.

Let's start with your phone. It sounds silly, but how many applications do you have open? Which apps are they? What level of interaction do they demand? Are your notifications on? Do they need to be? How many unread texts or emails do you have? How many total apps are on your phone? If we were to check your screen time usage on a daily basis, how many minutes (let's be real—hours) are you logging every day?

Take a look at your computer or laptop. Apply the same question: How many apps or programs are you running? If I were to "tab" through all your open items, how many would I have to get through to get me back to the one I started on? What about browser tabs? Tell the truth.

What other sources of information are around right now? Are you listening to a podcast or an audiobook? Is a TV on in the background? You may have a *Wall Street Journal* folded perfectly on your desk, next to a few magazines and a stack of unopened mail, all unread.

So now that we've taken a rough inventory of all the possible inputs, how do you feel? Add in our scattered attention between social media, news sites, mobile games, and communication applications, and we get a better understanding of what may be contributing to our overwhelm.

I often shut off my phone and laptop when I'm feeling overloaded to physically limit my inputs—no texts, calls, or emails. No app notifications of any kind. It allows me to get a bit of perspective and focus on my more important tasks and projects.

Once I've made some progress on important tasks and I don't have people pinging me every second, I've cleared space to focus more deeply and reframe the things that are in front of me. I have enough mental space for something like reading, which I love. When I'm in overwhelm, reading can turn into a "task," and it loses its appeal. It's a canary in my overwhelm coal mine. When reading becomes a chore, I know I'm in trouble. By limiting my inputs and giving myself enough mental space, I can once again take solace and joy in reading. What's your canary?

What would happen if you turned off every electronic device in your house for an hour? If you can't turn them off, what if you put them in airplane mode or "Do Not Disturb" mode? What if you shut down the notifications from LinkedIn and TikTok, from Slack or Teams?

Once you've reviewed the notifications and sheer number of applications or screens that you're working on, the next step is to drill down into the content you're regularly consuming and understand why.

During the pandemic, I asked clients to moderate their consumption of news. People wanted to regain a sense of control during that time through constant news monitoring. While information was important, critical information did not change every twenty minutes. That frequency of checking for updates was overstimulating and doing way more harm than good, so we set limits on news intake, either to a total number of minutes or the number of times to check it per day.

We also discussed where we sourced our information. What websites are you visiting? What social media accounts are you following? How are they making you feel? What information do they give you that you can take action from? When we're in overwhelm or burnout, remember that we're too open. Limiting our inputs allows us to focus on the tasks at hand, which will help to alleviate some of that feeling of inundation.

Taking a good look at where you get information and what types of information you access. This is not a judgment on any specific type of media. You may go to a pop-culture/celebrity blog to relax between meetings or after work. How long are you spending on this site? How is it helping or hurting you in terms of focusing on the tasks at hand? Is it a place to relax or a place to distract (and they don't always need to be the same thing)? Maybe you're a "true crime" junkie. If watching true crime drama is sending your nervous system into fight-or-flight mode, even if you enjoy it, consider taking a break for a while.

You don't have to cut yourself off from the world. I'm not saying you can never zone out on social media. But if you're trying to get yourself from the depths of overwhelm back up to the surface where you can begin to create space for inspiration, pick your sources of information and how often you interact with them more carefully. Be mindful and exercise restraint for your own benefit.

The goal isn't perfection. You don't have to turn into a digital monk or delete every app from your phone (unless you want to—there's something to be said for the people who still carry old school flip phones). This is about awareness and creating the time of quiet that allows you to hear your own thoughts again. Once you stop the noise, you can hear what truly matters.

If overwhelm is caused by too many inputs, then the antidote is having not just fewer but better and smarter inputs. We can't do it all, read it all, or fix it all, but we can decide what matters most and focus our attention on that. That's the magic of prioritizing. You get to call it.

EXERCISES

For You: Your Information Audit

1. **The Twenty-Four-Hour Input Inventory:** Track every information source you consume for one full day: apps, notifications, social media, emails, news, podcasts, videos. For each input, note: Did it energize or drain you? Did it help you focus or scatter your attention? Rate each on a simple keep/pause/eliminate scale.

2. **The Three-Change Challenge:** Based on your audit, make three immediate changes: Turn off one category of notifications, unfollow/unsubscribe from five sources that don't serve you, and establish one daily "input-free" hour. Start small but make it meaningful—even thirty minutes of quiet can be transformative.

For Your Team: Communication Streamlining

1. **Platform Audit:** Map all your team's communication channels (Slack, email, Teams, texts, etc.). Identify where people feel most overwhelmed by communication and where you're duplicating efforts across platforms. Discuss ways to modify your communication channels.

2. **Communication Charter:** As a team, create clear agreements about what gets communicated where, establish "No Notification" time blocks, and set expectations for uninterrupted work time. Make this agreement visible and revisit it monthly to ensure it's working.

12

THE ART OF RUTHLESS PRIORITIZATION

Have you ever remodeled a room in your home? You have an idea of what you want to fix, a vision for what you'd like the remodeled room to look like, and a set amount you can spend on the project. The remodel goes smoothly until construction starts and reality sets in. The tile you fell in love with costs double what you budgeted. The original sink you bought is on backorder, so you buy one that's more expensive but in stock. There's room in your budget to absorb the added costs, until the contractor finds a leak underneath your floor. Now your subfloor needs to be replaced, which blows your spending limit. You have two choices: You can either exceed your budget or prioritize which features matter most to you.

The same is true for creating spaciousness when we feel overwhelmed. When we're overloaded, we don't need more options and possibilites; we need focus.

We have to shrink our world to open it up.

In the last chapter, we started with an information diet—the first step in limiting what gets access to our attention. Our next step is narrowing our metaphorical field of vision, which we do through prioritization.

Even after taking time to limit our inputs, what remains on our plate can still seem both overwhelming and never-ending.

Begin with the most basic filter. Start by taking an honest look at what truly needs to get done vs. the things you'd like to get done. Yes, it's a need-vs.-want exercise, and sometimes those can be tricky.

Let's say you've got a busy Saturday planned. One of the kids has dance tryouts, you're got a Kilimanjaro-sized mountain of laundry to do, and you'd like to get the garage cleaned out and organized in time for the block party next weekend. What's a *need* vs. a *want*? If you're having trouble determining which is which, ask yourself what happens if the task doesn't get done. What are the implications, how serious are they, and how immediate?

If your kid doesn't make it to tryouts, there's no other chance for them to make the team, and dance is important to them. Tryouts are a need. If the laundry doesn't get done, you may run out of clothes. Push comes to shove, you could make a run to the store for a pack of clean underwear and socks in an emergency, but that's not ideal. Maybe you make it to base camp on the mountain of laundry—a load of underwear. The garage has been a small disaster for weeks. If it continues to be a disaster for the block party, you either keep the garage door closed or you give yourself grace that there are more important things on your list.

The distinctions can be harder to spot at work. I worked with a client, let's call him Edgar, who was feeling overwhelmed because of the rapid growth of his company. He had been scaling slowly, one client at a time, when word of mouth about his services started to spread. Suddenly he was in high demand, and he had a few challenges to overcome. First, because he was still so involved in the day-to-day operations, including taking on a fair amount of client work himself, he was the bottleneck in his own organization. Second, he was looking to create a new product that would be the perfect complement to his existing services but was finding it difficult to find time to work on the product. Third, while he had most of his internal processes well-documented, they weren't organized in a way he found useful.

We started with a want-vs.-need analysis. We knew that client work was paramount—a need. If he didn't serve his existing clients well, Edgar could lose their business along with the strong referral business he was starting to grow. But we also knew that Edgar couldn't do it all, so we decided to create a list of tasks and projects, in order of priority, and begin to delegate those tasks. While the new product was important because it wasn't out in the market yet, it was more of a want than a need. Nothing would happen in the immediate future if he continued to postpone product development. As for the processes that were documented but not organized, those also fell into a "want." The processes themselves had been created, honed, and captured, and those were needs. How they were organized, aside from having small potential impacts on productivity, was not important enough to fall into the "need" category.

When we're honest and diligent in categorizing the implications of something on our to-do list getting done or not getting done, we find our immediate needs are actually very few. Often our overwhelm is quasi-self-imposed.

We choose to continue to add to these long lists, the lists contribute to hijacking our nervous system, mashing together our wants and our needs, and suddenly everything is a need and we find ourselves spinning. That's why it's a good practice to start by separating projects and tasks into those two categories.

Once we've separated wants from needs, we can prioritize our tasks further. One of my favorite prioritization methods is the Eisenhower matrix. Created in 1954 by Dwight D. Eisenhower and popularized by Stephen Covey in 1989, this tool helps you to prioritize tasks and projects by both urgency and importance using a vertical axis of importance and a horizontal access of urgency. The top-right box contains tasks that are both urgent and important.

These tasks or projects have deadlines. The top-left box contains tasks that are important but not urgent, which can often be scheduled for a later date. The lower-left box houses urgent tasks that are not important. Think of things that must get done, but someone else has the skillset to do them. These tasks can be delegated. Finally, the lower-right box holds tasks that are both unimportant and not urgent— also known as distractions. We can also categorize these four boxes as: do it, decide when, delegate, and delete.

Eisenhower Decision Matrix

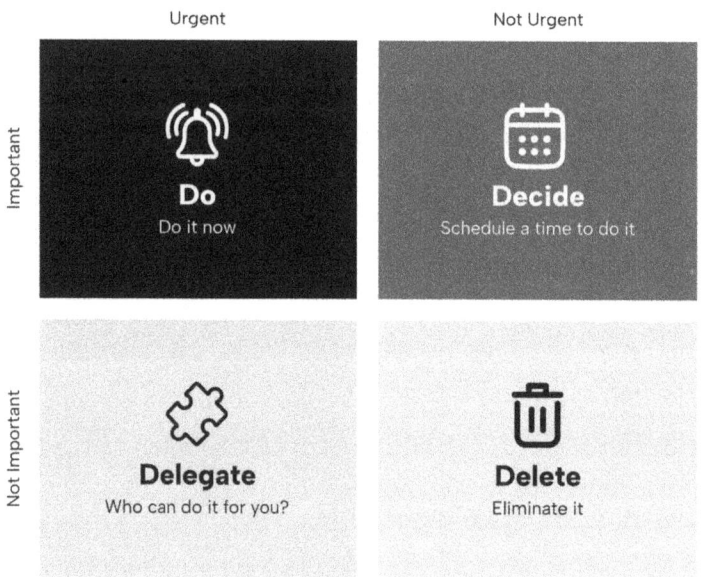

To use the matrix, take all of the open items on your to-do list, whether they are strategic projects like re-forecasting a budget or more task-oriented items like returning an email, and place them in one of the four quadrants of the matrix. Let's check out what could or should be in each box:

Urgent/Important:

These should be your immediate to-dos. Most of the items here have an upcoming deadline and a fairly serious consequence if not completed in time. Think taxes. Safety reviews. Calls from the media. Legal issues. A family emergency. Power outages. Company website or phone outages. Getting your car towed when you're broken down on the side of a freeway. A crying baby. These are just some of the things that can populate this quadrant. (And take care of the baby before filling out the matrix.)

In your first attempt at an Eisenhower matrix, you may find that your Urgent/Important quadrant is bursting with tasks and to-dos. Your anxiety, especially in overwhelm, has a tendency to flood this quadrant with nonurgent things that you think are urgent in the moment. Once you take a closer look at what you consider urgent, your Urgent/Important quadrant gets much smaller.

Employees, family, or friends may also try to fill this quadrant with tasks. However, because something may be urgent for them doesn't necessarily make it urgent for you. In all cases, you need to ask, "What happens if this doesn't get done right now?" If the answer doesn't involve something going immediately and seriously awry, it's probably not in the right quadrant.

When you're in overwhelm or burnout, it's critically important to hold the line because tasks in this quadrant take up a disproportionate amount of mental space. The cleaner you can keep this quadrant, the greater your ability to manage overwhelm.

Let's say you've narrowed your Urgent/Important category to just a few critical items. Despite having these tasks or projects in front of you, when you look at your longer daily to-do list, you haven't made any progress on them.

I can't tell you the number of times I've created a top three list of the most important things I know need to get done—and yet they are literally the last things for me to get to, if I get to them at all.

I want to address any potential shame or embarrassment that some of us have when we're reading Urgent/Important and realize that we ordered more bags of our favorite coffee online but didn't get any work done on our annual budget (and yes, while the coffee was worth it and certainly urgent should you run out, I will make the argument it's not so important).

Urgent/Not Important:

Items on this list have shorter deadlines, but they're not important enough for you to be putting your limited time and energy into them because they displace the important but not urgent. These tasks should be delegated. This works for home too. Remember the Mount Kilimanjaro of laundry? You've got wet underwear sitting in the washer. Certainly, you can be the one to flip it to the dryer or clothesline, but you could easily ask someone else in the household to do it. Running low on coffee? Urgent? Potentially. Important? Probably not.

The best way to determine if something can or should be delegated is by asking yourself if the task is something that truly only you can do based on your knowledge, skills, or understanding. If the answer is yes, it stays in the urgent/important box. If the answer is no and someone else can do this task, delegate it. Delegating can be frustrating. You might really like running payroll, or sending out meeting notes, or running that weekly meeting. You may love ordering coffee. Maybe you even love flipping laundry. But I would be willing to bet that someone else can do it. And before you tell me all the reasons why you are the best at it, which may or may not be true, the question remains: Is this a task that *only* you can do? If you're trying to save yourself from drowning in the sea of overwhelm, you need to reach for the life raft instead of sinking due to undelegated tasks.

Not Urgent/Important:

Tasks in this quadrant have a longer-lasting impact or are important in your greater strategy. If you're a New Year's resolution or annual goal setter, these are the next steps you need to do or habits you need to create to reach those goals. Personal examples could include anything from going to yoga three times per week, or meditating five times per week, to taking surfing lessons or reading one book a month. At work, tasks in this quadrant might include spending time on product strategy, talent review, or your communication cadence with your team or your board. The items on this list deserve your time and energy but not necessarily in a frantic, urgent manner.

Going back to Edgar's dilemma, he had two remaining big items: product development and organization. We decided that product development fell into not urgent/ important.

Tasks or projects in this quadrant can also be delegated using the same "do only what you can do" filter.

Another client, Sara, was in the middle of implementing a company-wide training platform. It was a large project that was time-consuming and complicated but once complete would have an enormously positive impact on the organization.

Like any big project, it hit hurdles and snags. And as the CEO, her time was best spent working with her leadership team to navigate those rather than jumping in and fixing the problems herself. She knew how important it was for her to learn to delegate— exponentially so while in burnout mode. This is part of a bigger theme of letting go and narrowing scope. She was able to take the things off her plate that others could do, which let her narrow her attention to complete only the things that (a) she was capable of doing and (b) that needed to be done.

Not Urgent/Not Important:

Items that are neither urgent nor important shouldn't be done at all. When we looked at Edgar's final task, "organizing processes," it fell into this category. Based on everything else that Edgar had going on, spending any time organizing processes was more counterproductive than productive. But to Edgar, because he likes order and organization, this task felt good, which is why he continued to add it to his Urgent/Important list.

I'm going to ask a question here, and you need to be honest with yourself. I will throw myself under the bus first, so feel free to join me. How often are you adding things to your to-do list because you know they're easy and you can have the satisfaction of checking them off? No shame here—I do it too. Especially if I'm overwhelmed . . . because that little sense of accomplishment I get with a check mark makes me feel like I'm making the smallest dent in my staggeringly high pile of work.

The challenge is that often that little item has little to no impact on our larger and more pressing priorities. While it feels amazing that I cleaned out a section of my closet, it doesn't get the proposal that's due next week any closer to being done.

I often ask clients to create a Top Ten Do NOT Do list. If you are tempted to drop into working on payroll instead of trusting your finance and HR team to do it, it goes on the list. If cleaning out your closet is a go-to activity when you're in overwhelm or high stress, it goes on the list. Any tasks that are not important and may actively hinder you from getting one of your more important items done should go away.

If the Eisenhower matrix feels too overwhelming or too confining, there's another way to think about prioritization.

In James Patterson's book *Suzanne's Diary for Nicholas*, one of the characters talks about juggling five balls, each of which represents something important in life: family, friends, work, health, and integrity. Patterson mentions that the balls can be made of rubber or glass. If we drop a glass ball, it will shatter. If we drop a rubber ball, it will bounce. My colleague Francine Lasky has added a third type of ball—a wooden ball. If you drop it, the wooden ball won't break, but as opposed to the rubber ball that bounces right back to you, the wooden ball takes some effort to pick up.

Which of your work balls is made of rubber that you can drop them and they'll just bounce right back up? These might be filling out an expense report or updating your CRM. These are also often balls that can be delegated. If they're going to bounce back if you drop them, does it matter who drops them? You may as well hand those off.

The wooden balls are more complicated to pick up, requiring more effort, and they may have a dent or a scratch depending on where you drop them from, but they will survive. Mentoring your high-performance employees or staying current on industry trends are examples of wooden balls.

And then we have the glass balls—if they break, they can't be repaired.

Key client relationships, critical project deadlines, trust with your team—all are examples of glass balls.

Most of the time, the glass balls remain the glass balls. There are very few of them, and regardless of what season or work or life we're going through, they tend to remain the same.

But the wooden and rubber balls may shift and change. While payroll was a wooden ball today, you may have built a backup process so it transforms into a rubber ball. Or perhaps new leadership at a long-time vendor doesn't know or trust you yet, turning a ball that once bounced to wood until you can rebuild the trust with their team and the ball morphs back to rubber again.

Whatever tool you use, the act of prioritizing both what's immediately in front of you and what you want your life to look like over time is a powerful way to gain spaciousness. It helps to quiet the noise, clarify your focus, and remind you what truly matters. From there we can go even deeper, turning inward to explore thoughts, patterns, and insights shaping how we move through the world.

EXERCISES

For You: The Priority Reality Check

1. **The Eisenhower Deep Dive:** List all current to-dos and place them in the matrix. Then look at your "Urgent/Important" box. What happens if each item doesn't get done today? Be brutally honest about what's truly urgent vs. what anxiety is making feel urgent.

2. **The Glass Ball Assessment:** Using the rubber/wooden/glass ball framework, categorize your current responsibilities. Identify your three to five glass balls (the nonnegotiables that will shatter if dropped). Everything else gets questioned: Can it be delegated? Delayed? Deleted entirely?

For Your Team: Collective Priority Alignment

1. **Team Glass Ball Agreement:** Have each team member identify their top three glass balls, then align as a group on the team's collective glass balls for the quarter. What are the three to five things that absolutely cannot be dropped without serious consequences?

2. **The Delegation Audit:** Map out all recurring team tasks and ask: "Who is the only person who can do this?" Anything that doesn't have a specific skill/knowledge requirement gets moved to a delegation list.

   Bonus: Create a shared "Do Not Do" list of tasks that feel productive but distract from glass ball priorities.

13

THE POWER OF THE PAGE

I have been a sporadic journaler my entire life, partly because I never really understood what journaling was. Starting with those early elementary school diary entries, I'd write down a catalog of my day without going deeper. The latch-hook pillow I brought for show-and-tell. The weather that was warm enough to wear shorts. The excessive mayonnaise my best friend's mom put in her tuna sandwiches. My diary was less about sharing my deepest secrets and dreams or making sense of the world through writing and more about taking stock.

As I grew older and switched out my "childish" diary for a journal, my journal entries didn't change dramatically.

My tactical, surface-level, stock-taking journaling wasn't helping me tackle the present or the future. There were no lists of to-dos, and it wasn't a place for worries or overwhelm or where I dumped all the trash of my brain on a piece of paper. It was just a recording of the things that had already happened.

I also feared that what I'd write would sound stupid, as though someone would read those journals. Including me. Would I be embarrassed just by reading them? Would someone else? I'd watched a lot of movies and read a lot of books in which someone "finds the journal and reads it," and there was always some sort of hell to pay as a result. So I held back.

I approached the page less as a sanctuary and more as a stage.

When you're trying to work out what's been troubling you, fears or doubts or dreams, writing only about what you think you "should" write about isn't helpful. It may be calming to move your hand across a page or take a break from a screen, but you're not accessing the true power of journaling.

I only started journaling in earnest when I hit my late twenties and my mental health took a hit, and I was scrambling to manage a new marriage, grad school (the campus was two hours away), and a full-time job.

You know what they say about necessity as the mother of invention—100 percent true. I wasn't journaling because I wanted to; I was journaling because I *needed* to. My brain was like a basket overflowing with tangled yarn, so full I didn't have enough space to work it all out.

That's when I finally understood the power of journaling. Used properly, it was like dumping that entire basket of tangled yarn out on a table. Through writing, I was able to get the knots undone and the yarn sorted.

When you're feeling overloaded, having a way to sort the yarn in your brain can be invaluable. Journaling can give you both perspective and mental space.

Sometimes when I mention journaling as a tool to a client, I can instantly see the discomfort on their face. Journaling can feel foreign to people and somewhat fear-inducing. I've heard everything from "I don't know what to write about," to "That's silly," to "It's not productive." Sometimes even the word *journal* will throw people.

I've had much better results when I rebrand it. I've renamed journaling to written clarity sessions, executive reflection sessions, focus pages, or even insight briefings. If the word "journaling" makes you uneasy, use whatever word or phrase works for you.

There are fundamental aspects to these sessions. First, while I believe in the power of the pen and paper, and there's science to back that up, write with the tool that works best for you. If you can swing a pen and paper, great. If you're a keyboard jockey and that's the only horse you ride, great. Second, give yourself uninterrupted time to journal. Notice I didn't say unlimited time. You can do a clarity session in five minutes if you need to. Once you've got a little bit of time set aside and a method for writing, you're ready.

There are many different ways to journal. Below are three for you to experiment with.

The first type of journaling focuses on clearing general brain clutter to gain spaciousness. In *The Artist's Way*, Julia Cameron has her readers work on morning pages every day. Morning pages are three full pages, written longhand, of whatever comes to mind. These pages are not designed to be focused on the project you're working on or focused on anything at all. They're meant to allow you to plan your day, to dump a lot of the thoughts that may be keeping you preoccupied or unable to focus into a place that can hold them. In doing so, they clear the way for a more spacious mind.

The second form of journaling focuses on a specific issue or problem that you may be struggling with. Especially if you're feeling oversaturated, it may be hard for you to direct your thoughts, and when you go to put your mind to a specific issue, you're quickly distracted or exhausted. You also may run into the same mental roadblocks over and over again. Writing allows us to gain a new perspective and mental distance and spaciousness that allows for more clarity. Psychologist James Pennebaker has shown that journaling helps people "organize chaotic thoughts," which results in greater clarity.

When we give ourselves the time to write about a specific issue, we are naturally slowing our thoughts to allow our hands or fingers to keep up with our brains. We may see details and con-nections that we didn't when our thoughts were buzzing around in our brains. Write it all down, including what you're feeling about it, what your gut says, what your fears are, and what your ideal outcome would be.

Our ability to gain clarity by working through our thoughts and gut instincts (and sometimes this will morph into visual mapping too) can allow us to potentially access a line of thinking we couldn't get at otherwise.

Then there's the third form: gratitude journaling. Regularly reflecting on gratitude helps you to refocus and reframe the people and events in your life in a way that shifts your thinking and perspective about everything else—even those things that may feel challenging or bad.

Here is one way you may structure your journaling, especially if you choose to do it at night. It can be a nice bookend to morning pages should you choose to take those on as well. (Fair warning, these prompts start easy and get more challenging as you go.)

1. List three things that you accomplished that day. While this is not specific to gratitude, it does help with the feeling we can have while in an overwhelmed state that "we got nothing done."

2. Write down one thing you are grateful for that day. It can be something as broad as "freedom" or as small as the tiny ladybug you noticed crawling on a leaf.

3. Identify a specific person you're grateful for. It doesn't need to be someone you know personally. It can be the woman who held the door for you when your arms were full, or the person who let you merge on the highway. It could also be your partner or your child, a parent or a close friend.

4. Write a compliment to yourself. This can't be a BS compliment. It has to be something meaningful and authentic

that you'd say out loud to someone else. So yes, you may compliment a stranger on their shirt, but that's not what we're looking for here. Here's how it could make sense: Maybe you wore an amazing shirt today, but the compliment to yourself is about looking put together and how that helps build your confidence. Maybe you've been working on managing your anxiety, so a compliment about how you handled yourself in an anxiety-provoking situation would be perfect. The more specific the compliment, the better.

5. Write down one thing you let go of today. Did you let go of your need to be perfect? Or your need to know all the details? Did you let go of the tendency to be a glass-empty type person? Maybe you let go of your need to be right? Did you let go of your need to respond and instead chose to deeply listen?

Journaling, in all its forms—from clearing mental clutter, to working through challenges, to expressing gratitude—is one of the most effective ways to carve out spaciousness for yourself. It's a way to slow down, get curious, and let your thoughts and feelings unfurl on the page, giving you the clarity you need to move forward.

The past few chapters have been about rising from the depths of overwhelm and giving you tools to get your head above water. Now that we've calmed your nervous system and found more room to breathe, it's time to build practices that can reliably create a sense of spaciousness, not just in crisis but every day.

Let's dive into Part 3: Practicing Spaciousness, where we'll explore how to make room for clarity and inspiration to show up, even when life doesn't slow down.

EXERCISES

For You: Your Clarity Writing Experiment

1. **The Three-Type Trial:** Over the next week, try each type of writing for ten minutes: brain dump (write whatever comes to mind), problem-focused (pick one specific challenge), and structured gratitude (use the five-point framework). Notice which type gives you the most clarity or relief.

2. **The Insight Tracker:** After each writing session, jot down one word that captures how you feel (lighter, clearer, stuck, etc.) and note any surprises or "aha" moments. What patterns emerge about when writing is most helpful for you?

For Your Team: The Five-Minute Focus

1. **Team Clarity Sessions:** Start one team meeting per week with a five-minute individual writing exercise: "What's one work challenge that's been circling in your mind?" Follow with voluntary sharing of insights (not problems but what became clearer through writing).

2. **Decision-Making Enhancement:** Before tackling a complex team decision, have everyone spend three to four minutes writing their initial thoughts privately, then share. Assure everyone in the room of confidentiality so they feel safe to share their thoughts. Notice if the quality of discussion improves when people have had time to clarify their thinking on paper first.

PART 3

SPACIOUSNESS

14

BUILDING YOUR FIELD OF DREAMS: MAKING ROOM FOR WHAT MATTERS

You've surfaced. You've steadied your breath. You are no longer lying with your cheek against the sidewalk. You've cleared just enough room to see what's next.

Now the work shifts.

This next section is about deliberately building practices around spaciousness. Spaciousness isn't something we can wait around for, hoping it will appear in the cracks in between meetings or the slivers of time in between errands, chores, events, and sleep.

We have to *make* time.

We have to weave space into our daily, weekly, and seasonal rhythms so that inspiration has a place to land. We're building the field in *Field of Dreams*. The field has to be built before any game can take place.

Spaciousness isn't a single moment of relief. It's a practice of making room for what matters again and again. In this chapter, we're going to explore how to begin a spaciousness practice.

Where can we start to get more space in our life? Maybe you'll find space by ducking out of an invitation to a networking event you don't want to attend. Are you supposed to be at that networking happy hour in a few hours? Yes. Are you overrun and needing some downtime to catch your breath? Also yes. So skipping that event gives you back some spaciousness.

The first part of creating a spaciousness practice is setting boundaries. Sometimes we struggle with the line between boundaries and selfishness. We may have obligations we need to meet. Obligation is born of "need." We often confuse it with "should" or "want" as we know from the discussion about priorities. There are times when we show up for others before we show up for ourselves. Showing up at a school recital when we've had a rough day is important. Supporting a friend who's in the hospital at a time when we feel stretched thin is important. But those true obligations are few and far between.

Assuming we're not in a period of providing critical support for others, we take care of ourselves by prioritizing ourselves. Self-care gives us the spaciousness to fulfill our true obligations. We can't pour from an empty cup. Tending to ourselves makes it possible to tend to others.

Recently, I was wildly sick. Fever, body aches, headache, and a wicked cough. I felt terrible. The illness came on the heels of time I'd spent away. My schedule of client meetings was already going to be very tight for the month, and I wasn't sure when I was going to be able to reschedule people. I didn't want to disappoint clients. I didn't want people to think less of me, of my ability to "be strong," or possibly give the impression that I was flaky.

So I chose to work from home for the first two days I was home. I was pretty good at faking my way through the morning. By the time lunch hit, my symptoms were getting worse. It was hard to be present, and I was barely vertical. I met with my therapist Tuesday afternoon.

"No offense, but are you insane?" she asked.

"Not that I'm aware of?"

"So you're incredibly sick, you're showing up to client meetings fifty percent present at best, you have two solid weeks of facilitation ahead, and your body is so depleted you're having trouble sitting up. Do you want to put yourself in the hospital?"

Of course, the answer to that was no. She asked why I wasn't taking the time away from work, and I listed all of my reasons.

"Have you ever thought that maybe the more disappointing experience for your clients is to have their coach not truly show up for a session? That clients will realize that you're out of integrity with the spaciousness and self-care you're always preaching to them? That you're potentially impacting even more people by extending your illness by not taking the rest you need to heal?"

That honest truth felt like a kick to the shin, but she was right.

Committing to spaciousness requires us to step away so that our interactions with others are more impactful. We need that space to retreat. That time in the oven to bake and develop. Who wants to eat half-baked bread?

A spaciousness practice has three components: physical, mental, and in time. We'll cover each of these in greater detail over the course of the next several chapters with specific practices for each.

You'll find that some practices fit into multiple components. They may help create physical and/or mental spaciousness. The issue is less about which drawer we place them in our toolbox, and more about whether we make them available. They're all tools we can use to create a sense of spaciousness that can lead us to openness and inspiration.

When you're just emerging from overwhelm, a practice of any kind can feel like one more thing. Start with where you are. A spaciousness practice doesn't have to consume hours of your day. Some days it's going to be ten minutes and some days it's going to be more. Consistency of the practice is more important than the volume of time you spend in it.

Is there an ideal balance for the amount of space we give ourselves in our daily lives? Potentially. If we're trying to balance our lives on a fulcrum, the more stress or the bigger the challenges in front of us, the more spaciousness we'll need.

Balance isn't a permanent state, because that assumes that you can spend an equal amount of time between the things that matter most to you. Your time is rarely split equally. The pendulum is always in motion, and as humans, we're just trying to keep it from the extremes. It's like the pirate ship ride at the amusement park that swings side to side. When you get close to one extreme or the other is when your stomach is in your throat, your heart beats wildly, and you feel the most out of control. Just like anything else in life, there are times where you'll have more space and times when you'll have less. The key is making the space a priority, no matter how much of it you can gather.

For spaciousness in its purest and potentially one of its longer forms, think of an unplanned day. You have no appointments or meetings, no chores or errands or "have-to-dos." You can take the time to walk to the bookstore instead of driving. You can linger over your morning coffee and watch the sun stream in through the window. You are not creating lists of tasks, thinking about meetings or deadlines, trying to mentally time block your day based on what needs to get done.

Spaciousness happens first as a feeling and a frame of mind—the mental spaciousness mentioned earlier. It helps us to shift some of our perceived "have to's" to "want to's" or even "not do's." Let's go back to the laundry example from the chapter on prioritization. Is there laundry in the hamper? Yes. (Maybe the better question is, When *isn't* there laundry in the hamper? But I digress.) Will the world cease to exist if the laundry is not washed today? No. Will not doing laundry potentially give us a little bit of anxiety? Potentially. Might we have to dig deeper in the closet for something to wear? Yes. Will skipping laundry give us some time and spaciousness back? Also yes. The same thing can be said about almost any chore. Will freedom fall if you don't make it to the grocery store today? I promise you, it will not. You may have breakfast for dinner or need to order take out, but the free world will remain intact.

Spaciousness doesn't happen by accident. It also does not require achieving a perfect balance or creating a life with no demands.

Practicing spaciousness is choosing, again and again, to make room for what matters in whatever way possible. Some days that space will feel expansive, like an unplanned morning with nowhere to be. Other days it will be five sacred minutes carved from the edge of a crowded calendar.

What matters is that we claim it. That we stop waiting for it to appear, and instead we make it happen.

In the chapter ahead, we'll explore how to build spaciousness into our daily, weekly, and seasonal rhythms. Because inspiration doesn't ask for perfection—it asks for room to breathe.

QUIZ

Before we dive into specific practices, let's take a moment to check in. This isn't about right or wrong answers; it's a way to notice where you are right now.

1. **When do you tend to create space for yourself?**
   a. In micro-moments—I'll grab a deep breath, a quiet pause, or a mindful sip of coffee when I can.
   b. Mostly in bigger chunks—vacations, retreats, long walks when I'm on the verge of burnout.
   c. Both! I try to weave in both smaller resets and plan larger resets too.
   d. Honestly? I don't create space; I stumble into it.

2. **Where do you think you are on the spaciousness spectrum?**
   a. I'm stuck in reactivity. I rarely feel as though I have any space.
   b. I catch some space here and there, but it's not consistent.
   c. I actively create spaciousness in my life—I block it, protect it, and return to it often.
   d. I have such little time for spaciousness, I don't think I'm even on the spectrum.

3. **If you had to choose your next move, it would be:**
   a. Start small—find one daily moment where I can pause (like at the end of meetings or before opening an email).
   b. Carve out a bigger block—maybe block a half-day or plan a simple personal retreat.
   c. Both—I want to create both smaller and bigger moments of reset.
   d. All of the above?

4. **What's your biggest barrier to creating spaciousness?**
   a. Guilt—I feel selfish taking the time for myself when others need me or there's work to be done.
   b. Fear—I worry that if I slow down, everything will fall apart or I'll fall behind.
   c. Habit—I'm so used to being busy that I don't know how to be still or what to do with quiet time.
   d. Logistics—I genuinely don't see where I could find the time in my current schedule.

5. **When you do find spaciousness, what tends to happen?**
   a. I get anxious or restless and fill it back up with tasks or distractions.
   b. I crash—I sleep, zone out, or do nothing because I'm so depleted.
   c. I feel creative, inspired, or more connected to what matters to me.
   d. It varies—sometimes I rest, sometimes I get energized, depending on what I need.

What your answers mean:
If you selected mostly A's or D's, you're ready to start building intentional micro-spaciousness because tiny pauses can change everything. Pay attention to guilt patterns (question 4) and notice if you're filling space out of habit (question 5).

If you selected mostly B's, you may benefit from bringing macro-spaciousness into your life more consistently and working through fears about slowing down.

If you selected mostly C's, keep nurturing your spaciousness practice and ask yourself how you can protect it even more fiercely while helping others in your life understand its value.

15

PERMISSION SLIPS

Creating space is one thing. Using it is another.

Even when we carve out time, set boundaries, or build practices that give us breathing room, something inside us can still resist.

We may feel inspiration more easily at conferences or during retreats. That's partly because we're free from our day-to-day worries, even though they haven't gone away. We are not confronted with the check engine light when we start the car, the credit card bill that was higher than we'd expected, the nagging voice in the back of our minds about scheduling that medical appointment.

At a conference or retreat, we create mental distance between our "normal" life and the time and place where we are now, allowing us to be present in the moment. That distance insulates us from outside stress and quiets the voice of our internal Judge (who we'll meet later in the book).

So how do we create this space in our daily lives? More important, how do we allow ourselves to create this space in our daily lives?

We give ourselves permission.

Because normally the hardest person to get permission from . . . is ourselves.

Giving ourselves permission feels way easier when we're out of town and not in our regular routine. It's harder when we're back home in the thick of our daily grind.

It's also harder to do when you feel like creating space is unnecessary. (Trust me, this practice is necessary if you want to be inspired or fulfill a role in which you inspire others.)

We feel perfectly fine giving permission to others. We're happy to allow them the time and space they need to recover, to reconnect, to rejuvenate themselves, but we feel obligated to keep pushing, telling ourselves we don't need or potentially deserve spaciousness.

For those of us who may be rule-followers, people-pleasers, or hyper-achievers, the grace we so easily extend to others is difficult to extend to ourselves. Sometimes we seek permission from those around us. We want to know that it's all right to step away from email and go to the pool to swim laps in the middle of the day or take the trip with the family even though we have a big project launching at work. We look to others to give us their blessing and support, allowing us to create the space we need to refill our own cups.

For those of us who are servant leaders, it can seem especially daunting to put our needs in front of those we serve—whether in our organizations, our communities, or our own homes.

We are the ones creating the excuses, the justifications, the laundry list of reasons why we can't make time to create space.

And with those excuses and justifications often comes a few emotions. Shame. Guilt. Fear. The voice that whispers, "You should be doing more. You should be somewhere else. You should be someone else."

How do we quiet that voice?

We can start with a simple but powerful exercise.

In *Braving the Wilderness*, Brené Brown recounts the time she was guesting on the *The Oprah Winfrey Show* for the first time. Nervous about appearing on the show, Brené wasn't sure what to do. She remembered before she left home she'd written a permission slip for her daughter to go on a field trip. Brené decided to do the same thing for herself— write herself a permission slip that allowed her to be silly and present and her true authentic self with Oprah and to let the nervousness go. That small but pivotal exercise allowed her to lean in, be present, and enjoy her time on the show.

One silver lining I saw come out of the pandemic with my clients was their shift in perception around time, specifically time spent at home with friends and family. One CEO went from working fifteen-hour days in the office to spending every lunch hour playing with his two daughters, making chalk drawings on the driveway and riding scooters. During this time, the stress was higher than ever for him as he was trying to run a company during a pandemic while also in the process of selling that company. Tom's normal MO would have been to work even harder, spend more time at the office, more time on the laptop. But instead, he gave himself permission to spend lunch with his daughters every day. They drew hopscotch boards and castles, they drew giant daisies and family portraits. They raced scooters and made ramps and jumps. The time with his kids helped to balance him out, refocused him on the why of what he was doing, and helped him to let go of the smaller, inconsequential things he may have spent hours laboring about and worrying over in the past. This time and space he allowed himself also gave him insights he wouldn't have had about positioning the company for sale and about the transaction itself.

Giving ourselves permission isn't selfish or indulgent. It's necessary.

Without it, the space we work so hard to create stays empty, like a door we've unlocked but never opened. Permission slips are small, simple tools, but they can quiet the inner voice that tells us we don't deserve rest, space, or ease, or that spaciousness isn't a necessary component for inviting inspiration.

Whether it's a few minutes away from your desk or a longer pause to reconnect with what matters most, what you're really granting yourself is permission to show up fully and the permission to allow your brain the space it needs to grab onto a lightning bolt of inspiration.

EXERCISES

For You: Your Personal Permission Practice

1. **The Permission Slip Experiment:** Write yourself a permission slip for one specific way you'll create spaciousness today. Use this format: "Today I give myself permission to . . ." Keep it visible and notice what internal resistance comes up—what voices try to talk you out of it?

2. **The Permission Check-In:** At day's end, reflect: What did honoring your permission slip allow you to feel, notice, or create? What would have been different if you hadn't given yourself that permission? Notice the ripple effects of that spaciousness.

For Your Team: Collective Permission Culture

1. **Team Permission Round:** Have each person write a permission slip for creating space in their work week that could support better thinking or creativity. Share them (if comfortable) and notice common themes—what permissions do your team members most need to give themselves?

2. **Permission Follow-Up:** The following week, check in: How did honoring those permission slips impact work quality, creativity, or team dynamics? What did you notice about productivity when you created space vs. when you didn't? Use insights to establish team norms around protecting thinking time.

16

LETTING GO

One client was working his way up to the CEO role in his company. It had been Brian's longtime dream to lead an organization. He made a series of sacrifices over the years to keep himself on that path. In addition to spending at least half his time on the road, Brian worked weekends and nights, took every job he was offered, and moved his family from one city to the next. Leadership told him he was well on his way to the C-level, and Brian kept his head down and continued grinding.

Many positions later and on the brink of the promotion he thought he'd always wanted, Brian allowed himself something he hadn't in many years—a two-week vacation. He completely unplugged during that time: no work calls, meetings, or email.

During that break, Brian realized he valued his time more than the status he'd been chasing. He had all the money he needed, the title, the house—he had achieved "enough." The time away helped him to see that his current life hadn't really allowed him time away from the job and that the next level of responsibility would require him to sacrifice even more of his personal life. He had to let go of an old dream that no longer suited him. Holding on to a dream can take up psychic real estate. Brian chasing the C-suite dream crowded out his other longings, values, and joys.

Brian took a few months to pivot to a completely different career, one that gave him more time and flexibility, in addition to allowing him to follow a passion he'd kept hidden for years. The space Brian gave himself during that two-week period led to an insight and inspiration to start a completely new life.

That lesson, the counterintuitive power of release, is one I've had to learn again and again. We think control will save us. That if we just grip tighter, dig deeper, zoom in closer, we'll find the solution. And sometimes that's true. Scrutiny and effort can carry us a good way along, but not always. Because the tighter we grip, the smaller our field of vision becomes. We can't see what's beyond the problem we're trying to solve. We can't even see the right problem to solve.

One of the most challenging aspects, and most antithetical, of setting the stage for inspiration is that it requires us to let go. We are so accustomed to gripping more tightly, to becoming more granular on a problem to understand it or solve it. We feel like if we can just put it under a microscope to see "what's really going on" or if we can just tighten the reins a little more, we can better control it.

Inspiration is not required to solve the tough stuff.

But here's why inspiration is important.

Letting go creates the space for inspiration. It allows new ideas, new possibilities, and yes, sometimes a feeling of relief to enter. It opens the door when logic has us locked inside.

Letting go comes in many forms. Let's start by looking at what can happen when we choose to let go of control.

Jim runs a high-end landscaping firm and was concerned because he was losing one of his best leaders and top-performing employees. Jim's company had just signed a large contract with a client, and this employee was going to play a critical role in the project that had just been signed. This employee led a large division within the organization, and he and Jim were also currently in negotiations to become partners.

Jim had recently purchased the company from the former owner. Initially, the sale was going to be made to both him and

Sam, the employee who was at risk of leaving. Based on Sam's financial situation, he wasn't able to participate in the initial sale. Jim felt strongly that post-sale, he wanted to become business partners with Sam.

Jim and Sam began negotiating how that would happen. They'd have a conversation, Jim would feel like he understood what Sam wanted and would have his attorney incorporate it into the agreement. But when he and Sam would sit down again with a revised agreement, the conversation would derail.

Sam was becoming more distant, and Jim was perplexed. He felt he was meeting all the needs Sam voiced. He'd found an attorney for Sam to use. Sam and Jim were still getting along in the daily running of the business, but talks broke down around the partnership, and Sam let Jim know that he was going to look for a job elsewhere. Jim went back to his notes, back to the agreement, back to the conversations they'd had and couldn't figure it out.

Jim is a member of a peer advisory board. The group is very good at giving members perspective and providing a space to open up to new ideas and ways of seeing specific issues.

With the help of his peers, he was able to see that Sam may not want to buy into the company. But Jim needed to let go of all the logic to see this. The redlined agreements. The cap tables. The loan language.

When Jim sat down with Sam to talk about nixing the partnership deal, Jim said the relief on Sam's face was evident. Sam felt pressured to pursue the partnership, but he didn't truly want to, which is why negotiations failed. By negotiating a new title and compensation plan without the burden of ownership, both Jim and Sam got what they wanted.

In letting go and allowing the advisory group to see the issue, Jim gained a different perspective. Instead of digging down into more of the logic, he found the answer by opening himself up to what else was possible.

When we grip tightly, like Jim did with his redlined agreements and logical approach, we crowd our mental space with details, plans, and contingencies. Our focus narrows, and we become consumed with managing, fixing, and controlling. In this case, Jim was managing, fixing, and controlling the wrong problem.

The spaciousness comes when we release the need to control every variable. The space lets in the perspective we couldn't access before. When we create this space for clarity, we stop trying to force a solution and start seeing possibilities we hadn't imagined. Inspiration often comes when we finally stop trying so hard to solve and instead start to see.

Sometimes creating space requires us to let go of a dream.

When you loosen your grip on older dreams, you clear the way for what lights you up now. Spaciousness in this way is both emotional and existential. It's the wide-open field that allows you to ask, "What matters most to me?"

Inspiration flows when we're aligned with the truest present-day version of ourselves.

Sometimes we need to let go of an identity.

I've had the same opportunity to learn how to let go over and over again.

My entire life was planned out by the age of thirteen. I dreamed of going to college, getting married, going back to school for an MBA, and working myself up the corporate ladder. At the same time, I knew I wanted to start a family, have three kids, live on the East Coast, and make CEO by my early forties. I spent those soft moments before sleep imagining the house and the job, the three kids running around with a dog in the big backyard, my parents' visits where my mom would teach my kids to craft just like she'd done with my brother's kids.

And it all worked—until it didn't. I married my college sweetheart, got the degrees, and was moving up the corporate ladder on the West Coast. Everything was going according to plan. But at the age of thirty-four, it all started to unravel. The first snag was that I couldn't get pregnant. We tried all the fertility options, and finally I was pregnant with twins. But a few weeks later, I lost the twins and my mom within a month of each other. My career halted. The move back east was put on hold. I recovered. I made changes.

Fast-forward another few years, I left my executive role, my marriage fell apart, and the house, the job, the kids, the yard, and my mom—were all gone.

The life I'd imagined for myself at the age of thirteen was a heap of burning wreckage down at the bottom of a ravine.

All of the labels I'd used to define myself: "daughter of," "wife of," "executive at," were gone.

I was terrified. Because everything I'd used to measure my success, to prove what I'd achieved, how I'd made my mark in the world, had slipped away. So who was I now?

I had told myself a lot of stories about what success should look like. Turns out those stories weren't true.

The more I explored this gap in my life (that felt like an abyss), the more I realized it wasn't really the life I wanted. Like Brian, I wanted my time back. My creativity. I wanted to become a different version of myself.

Without the constraints of who I thought I "should be," the world of possibility opened up for who I "could be."

My clients often hear me say, "The good news is that you have a choice. The bad news—is that you have a choice." I made the choice to let go of that version of me that thirteen-year-old Danielle had created. The version that no longer fit, that had me collapse inward instead of expand outward, that had made me smaller instead of allowing me to spread my wings.

Letting go of that outdated identity was hard. I clung to it until loss tore it from my hands. But letting go allowed me to create something new. To be a version of myself that fits with where I am now and where my interests lie. Because of that alignment with my interests, I also feel more easily inspired. The people, work, and activities I surround myself with open the door for inspiration.

The last form of letting go I'll cover is the letting go of perfectionism.

Suleika Jaouad, the bestselling author and creator of *The Isolation Journals* newsletter, knows this terrain well. In a *Fast Company* interview, she describes the moment she realized that perfectionism wasn't working for her. It wasn't making her braver or more creative; it was keeping her stuck. What she craved most wasn't flawless work; it was truth, connection, and creativity. But perfectionism crowded out the spaciousness she needed for those things to grow.

When Suleika began *The Isolation Journals*, first as a creative ritual during illness, then as a community project during the pandemic, she invited herself and others to let go of polished outcomes. Her prompt wasn't "Make something beautiful"; it was "Write. Draw. Reflect. Share."

In letting go of the need for everything to be "right," Suleika made space for what matters: the creative spark, the connection with others, the chance to be surprised by her own exploration and creativity.

That's the gift of letting go of perfectionism. Perfectionism is crowded with fear. By releasing the perfectionism, we clear the clutter so that inspiration can move freely.

Creating space isn't just choosing what to include; it's also deciding what we're willing to release.

We can carve out time, set boundaries, and write ourselves permission slips. But if we're still carrying the weight of old obligations, perfectionism, guilt, or control, the space we've made stays crowded. Spaciousness doesn't come only from adding more pauses or blocking more time. Sometimes it comes from lightening our load.

We lighten our loads by letting go of stories about ourselves, our lives, and our goals that no longer suit us.

Letting go allows us to step fully into the space we've created and to breathe deeper, think more clearly, and invite inspiration in.

EXERCISES

For You: Release and Receive

1. **The Grip Inventory:** Identify one area where you're holding on too tightly (a project, outcome, identity, or standard). Write down what you're afraid will happen if you let go, then explore: What might become possible if you loosened your grip even 10 percent?

2. **The Story Rewrite:** Notice one limiting story you tell yourself about who you should be or what success should look like. Complete this sentence: "Instead of believing I should be _____, what if I trusted that I could be _____?" Write out both versions and notice which feels more spacious.

For Your Team: Collective Release

1. **Team Grip Check:** Ask the team to identify one area where you're collectively holding too tightly—a process, timeline, perfection standard, or outdated strategy. Discuss: What are we afraid will happen if we let go? What innovation might emerge if we created more space?

2. **The 80 Percent Experiment:** Choose one area where the team typically aims for 100 percent perfection and experiment with 80 percent completion or "good enough." Track what gets freed up—time, energy, creativity—and what new possibilities emerge as a result.

17

POP YOUR HELIUM HAND

Do you suffer from "helium hand"?

Picture this—you're sitting in a meeting (leadership meeting, PTA meeting, family meeting, volunteer meeting, doesn't matter) and someone asks, "Who's willing to lead this initiative?" and no one moves a muscle. And you're looking around, wondering who's going to do it, and the more time passes, the more uncomfortable you become until all of a sudden, without realizing it, your hand is suddenly floating up off the table and into the air to volunteer. Sound familiar?

If that's the case, you, my friend, have helium hand.

A client introduced me to this term years ago, and I love it. She's a CEO and business owner, very involved in industry events and leadership, a wife and a mom, and she suffers from a chronic case of helium hand. We were talking about the overwhelm she was feeling implementing a new ERP in the business while balancing hiring, a new training system, a reorganization, and supporting an industry organization by drafting new bylaws—not to mention her responsibilities outside of work. And then she dropped the bomb that she'd just added chairing the annual fundraiser for her children's school to her plate. I asked her why she volunteered.

"Because I can do it, right? It's important for the school, and I can fit it in somehow."

Helium hand shows up not only at work but in volunteering to run a gala, coaching the T-ball team, planning the baby shower or the family reunion, regardless of how much time you truly have. Sometimes your helium hand may even show up in meetings with your direct reports. You notice they're feeling overwhelmed and can't take on any more, and so you take on the new initiative, or worse, you take on the work you'd already delegated.

When you're creating more time and space for yourself, you need to be far more diligent about how and where you use your time and energy. If you're in overwhelm and you know you need to narrow your focus, time management becomes that much more critical. As much as you may want to believe you can magically make more hours in your day, or that you have a super-human multitasking skill (spoiler alert: you don't), you need to both focus and limit your energy to the most important people and activities in your life.

For many overachievers and people-pleasers, helium hand is hard to overcome. I see helium hands floating up all over the place.

The hardest thing about helium hand? The intent behind it is almost always good.

You mean well. You want to do the right thing, support the cause, and if you're being honest, maybe there's a tiny part of you who's a people-pleaser or has a fear of disappointing others. You may even like being the hero. No judgment there.

Helium hand is often less about obligation and more about identity. We like being seen as the one who steps up, pitches in, and is always willing to help.

We convince ourselves that we can make room for whatever we've just signed up for, in addition to helping with homework, supporting an aging parent, onboarding a new member of the leadership team, and recommitting to date night once a week.

And that's all really beautiful . . . until we discover its true cost. The reality is that those commitments eat up the very space we need to think, breathe, and lead.

We overestimate the amount of time we have. Much of this stems from the fact that we're available at a moment's notice to anyone who reaches out to us, thanks to those little devices we carry with us everywhere. You can be at water polo practice and returning emails, on the commute home and talking on the phone, in line at the coffee shop and texting friends to organize a night out. Our time is already double-booked because of multi-tasking, and now we're trying to edge in just one more thing. When we add extra commitments, any minuscule margin of time we set aside for ourselves gets smaller and smaller.

What do you do when you feel like your helium hand may be on the rise, especially if you're already feeling short on space and time? Take out a figurative pin and pop it by saying no.

Maybe that pinprick sounds like, "Let me think about it and check my bandwidth and follow up with you tomorrow." Or it could also sound like, "I'd love to support this, but I'm at capacity and I don't want to say yes unless I can truly show up."

Helium hand doesn't just steal your time; it steals the air that inspiration needs to breathe. In order for great ideas to float into our brains, we need the mental space for them.

Every time you say "yes" out of habit or guilt, when your schedule is so packed and you feel obligated to do "one more thing," you edge out those moments of inspiration, often when you need them the most. You'll also be more efficient and creative with the things you currently have on your plate by limiting them. You've only got so much room in your belly, so don't fill your plate so high that it makes you sick.

The next time you feel that hand start to float, pause. Breathe. Picture the pin. And remember: Protecting your space isn't selfish; it's sacred.

EXERCISES

For You: Hand Management Strategy

1. **The Helium Hand Audit:** Reflect on the last ninety days—identify one commitment you wish you hadn't made. Ask: Why did my hand float up? What was the real cost (time, energy, spaciousness)? What would I have done with that space instead?

2. **The Pre-Commitment Protocol:** Before any meeting where volunteering is a possibility, decide on your response strategy. Write down your go-to phrase: "Let me check my bandwidth and get back to you tomorrow" or "I need to honor my current commitments first." Practice saying it until it feels natural.

For Your Team: Collective Hand Awareness

1. **Team Helium Hand Assessment:** Rate yourselves individually and collectively (1–10) on helium hand tendency. If scores are 6+, discuss: What's the culture cost of everyone always saying yes? How does constant overcommitment impact our core work quality?

2. **The Strategic No:** Identify one type of request your team consistently says yes to out of habit rather than strategy. Practice saying no as a team to protect collective bandwidth for your most important work. Maybe even role-play it in a meeting. Track what becomes possible when you stop filling every available moment.

18

THE CATHEDRAL EFFECT

Have you ever stood in a cathedral like Notre-Dame or Saint Peter's Basilica? The impossibly high ceilings, the space filled with light, and a sense of peace, all give us a feeling of elevation that comes with inspiration. As H. G. Wells once said, "A great cathedral is a proud and solemn thing; it inspires awe by its size, beauty and age . . . It sets the soul trembling with wonder and gratitude."

That sounds like mental spaciousness to me.

Designing for spaciousness means shaping our environments, both physical and mental, so that they naturally encourage clarity, creativity, and inspiration. We can create conditions where inspiration feels at home in environments where light, space, and structure work together. Even furniture layout can support or stifle our ability to think big and feel open. Let's begin with something ancient and universal—the cathedral effect.

First coined by Joan Meyers-Levy and Rui Zhu in an article published in the *Journal of Consumer Research* in 2007, the cathedral effect is the principle that our cognition follows our visual environment. Researchers studied the influence of ceiling height on the type of mental processing that people use. They found that higher ceilings prompted thoughts that were more expansive and creative, led to "big picture" thinking, and created a sense of openness and spaciousness. Conversely, lower ceilings created greater feelings of confinement, which were useful for increasing focus on more detailed, analytical, and precise work.

The study concluded that in a high-ceilinged environment, our language and ideas are more abstract, broader, and often future-focused. Higher ceilings are great for creative, strategic, and brainstorming exercises. Low ceilings support detailed work, such as accounting, spreadsheets, coding, etc.

In addition to encouraging more open-minded work, physical spaciousness also allows us to pull from broader swaths of memory. Why does this matter for inspiration? Because inspiration often emerges when we connect seemingly unrelated ideas, when we link a present challenge to a past experience, or when a memory unlocks a new way of seeing a situation. The more mental "territory" we can scan, the more raw material we have for creative connections. We don't just call on what's in front of us. We're more likely to recall a conversation from years ago, an article we read last month, or a childhood experience, all of which could help shape a new solution or spark a fresh idea.

Imagine your mind as a vast library filled with ideas, memories, knowledge, and connections. When you're in a small, low-ceilinged space (physically or mentally), it's like standing in a cramped aisle with your nose to the spine of a single row of books. Your focus narrows. You can see only what's right in front of you. That's useful when you need precision, like looking for a specific fact, checking details, or solving a clearly defined problem.

But when you step into a place that feels open, with high ceilings and light pouring in, it's like standing on the balcony of your own mental library. Suddenly you can see all the shelves at once. You spot connections between titles and authors, you remember books you forgot were there, and you can roam freely and allow your curiosity to guide you.

That's what the cathedral effect gives us—it lifts us up to a place where our mind can wander. The openness in our physical space loosens the boundaries in our cognitive space.

In one of his podcast episodes, Andrew Huberman, a neuro-scientist and tenured professor in neurobiology at Stanford, talks about the fact that when we are in spaces that are more open, our visual focus and attention naturally expand. When we're in tighter, smaller spaces, our focus constricts.

Doesn't that make sense? Architects have known this for centuries. What cathedral have you stepped into that didn't have high vaulted ceilings that brimmed with light and color? What museums, town halls, old courthouses didn't have wide-open entryways and grand ceilings? And what about symphony halls? Theaters? These venues are all designed to inspire us with what's happening inside of them, everything from sermons to civic services, from trials to operas. Yes, some of the design is for acoustics, but some of it is also about what the building represents and what people feel when they see or stand inside them. Expansive physical spaciousness can give us that sense of elevation, the greater depth and understanding we have when we feel inspired.

We can use this same principle in our personal lives. When you're getting ready to do big-picture thinking, whether individually or with your team, think carefully about where you host that session. If you're discussing things like values, three-to-five-year strategic plans, or mission statements, pick a location with higher ceilings, a sense of spaciousness, and more light pouring through the windows. If possible, having a view of the outside and nature can help. It may even make sense to book your lunch or breaks outdoors.

The same is true for your own inspirational sessions. Most of us don't have rooms in our houses with varying ceiling heights. If you do, go to your high-ceilinged room to do your loftier thinking sessions. If, as for many of us, ceiling height is uniform throughout your home, pick the room with the greatest sense of space and light and the least amount of clutter.

Not everyone has access to grand spaces. We may occupy a shared office or a cube without access to a window, a studio apartment, or a space without high ceilings or lots of light. That's okay. Spaciousness can also come from opening a window, adding a lamp, or simply changing where we direct our gaze.

The line of sight that picks up ceiling height and light will also potentially pick up visual obstacles, like clutter and other objects blocking your view. This isn't a request to clean your house, trust me (even though cleaning is a great excuse when you're trying to avoid focusing on whatever you have in front of you). Spaciousness can also come from what we subtract. Just move whatever is in your immediate area to a new place. Even shifting your gaze from a screen to the horizon will help. This is one reason why we tend to be more creative or engage in bigger-picture thinking in an unfamiliar place. When we're at home or in the office and our surroundings are familiar, the objects around us can summon a memory or a thought—whether it's a trip down memory lane or a reminder of something to add to a to-do list. In different surroundings, even a coffee shop down the street, we have fewer familiar visual distractions.

While the research backs up the idea that a less-cluttered space leads to a greater sense of spaciousness and higher likelihood of inspiration, history shows that spaciousness doesn't always require a clean and tidy desk. Einstein's office at Princeton was famously captured in a photograph with stacks of papers on his desk and books piled on top of each other in his bookcase. Frida Kahlo's home and studio at La Casa Azul was filled with a riot of color, artifacts, art supplies, and personal mementos. We also know that both Edison's workspaces in Menlo Park and Julia Child's kitchen had counters covered in prototypes and tools, or pots, pans, and cooking gadgets.

There's no wrong answer. Use what works for you.

The same is true for light. When the light is just right, it can make us bloom with joy and contentment. Different times of day can open the door for creativity, spaciousness, and inspiration. For some people, inspiration starts with the light of dawn creeping into their front room, while others relish the late afternoon when light pours in through their office window, or twilight, watching the sky turn the most delicate of purple and into a deep blue and then navy. Everyone has a different magic hour when they're most likely to feel inspired.

What matters is what this light does for our bodies, how the horizons it gives us mentally (whether in the light of day or the lack of horizon that stretches into the stars of the night sky) allow us to be more open to inspiration.

The cathedral effect also reminds us that spaciousness isn't just something we feel; it's something we can create. Our physical spaces shape our mental spaces. Where we work, where we pause, where we let our eyes rest: All of these influence how open, creative, and inspired we feel. You might find visual spaciousness simply by clearing your line of sight, shifting in your chair, or stepping outside for a breath of fresh air. The key is to notice and choose the environments that help you think bigger and connect more of those mental dots.

Next, we'll look at other ways to design spaciousness into your life so that when inspiration visits, it feels welcome to stay.

EXERCISES

For You: Space-Mind Connection Mapping

1. **Your Inspiration Geography:** During the next week, track when and where you feel most creative or get your best ideas. Note elements such as ceiling height, lighting, clutter level, indoor/outdoor, time of day. What patterns emerge in your optimal thinking environments?

2. **The Five-Minute Space Shift:** Choose one regular thinking task (e.g., planning your day, problem-solving, creative work)

and experiment with doing it in three different environments this week. Notice: How does your thinking change in a cluttered space compared to a clear one? Near a window vs. away from it? In your usual spot or somewhere new?

For Your Team: Strategic Space Design

1. **Meeting Environment Audit:** For the next month, alternate your strategic meetings between different spaces—conference room vs. outdoor space, high-ceiling area vs. typical meeting room, well-lit vs. dimly lit spaces. Track the quality of ideas and engagement in each setting.

2. **The Cathedral Meeting:** Plan your next big-picture session (e.g., strategic planning, vision work, problem-solving) intentionally. Choose the most spacious, light-filled location available. Compare the outcomes to similar meetings held in typical conference rooms—what differences do you notice in creativity and scope of thinking?

19

THE GREAT OUTDOORS EFFECT

If spaciousness has a birthplace, it might just be outside.

Nature offers the most literal kind of spaciousness— broad horizons, open sky, and a world free from walls, roofs, or most important, screens. When we step into nature, even briefly, we give our minds permission to stretch. As we widen our line of sight, something inside us also opens and expands.

People often feel inspired when they're out in nature, whether watching a sunrise crest a mountaintop or staring up at the canopy of a sequoia. We feel awe in that moment, which can also lead to a sense of inspiration.

In fact, in a recent survey I conducted, more respondents listed nature as their most inspiring space than any other location. There are a few reasons why this could be a universal truth.

When we're outside, our physical horizon is greater. Have you ever taken a bike ride around the area where you often drive? Do you notice how much more you see and experience? Your horizon is larger—there isn't any physical restriction like a car door or a hood or a roof limiting your line of sight. You become more fully immersed in your surroundings.

In his book *A Year in the Woods*, Torbjorn Ekelund wrote about his one-year challenge to spend one night a month in the woods. Each month, starting in January, he'd leave the comfort of his home and family and trek out to the Nordmarka forest not far from his home in Oslo to spend the night in nature.

His first month out he was woefully unprepared—winter in Norway is not a picnic. But he learned what he needed to be comfortable while out in the woods, and he was more prepared physically and mentally.

This wasn't a crazy trek. He wasn't hiking the Appalachian Trail or scaling the Matterhorn.

It also wasn't meant to be a test of physical and mental strength.

His goal was to take the time once a month to go to a place without man-made inputs. Without cell phones or laptops, without televisions or bluetooth speakers, without the sound of car engines or voices. He made a conscious choice to disconnect from those things. More important, it was an opportunity for him to broaden his horizons. To listen to the quiet of a snowfall, watch the scampering of a squirrel. It was about simplicity and spaciousness.

The beauty of his story isn't in some radical awareness he had about the impact of spending time alone in the woods. It's in the budding relationship that Ekelund builds with nature. As readers, we get to witness what it's like to be present: what he hears and sees, what he smells. He describes a gentle unfurling of his consciousness, his relationship to a specific place in nature and noticing how it changes through the season. His story was about noticing and being present.

It was also a study of making a habit of that connection, of prioritizing time, despite having a spouse and kids, a job and a busy life, to take time out for himself and create space.

Of course nature is inspiring. But it's different for all of us. Some of us do not have easy access to national parks and forests, or uninhabited deserts or mountains. We may live in a large city or a planned community in the 'burbs. We may live closer to nature but based on our upbringing may never have had a relationship with it. Sometimes we grow up in families that are not outdoorsy at all, and everything we know about the outdoors we learn from places like the local nature center or YMCA.

A dear friend has a gorgeous, tiered backyard that overlooks a canyon. She has trees and plants of all sorts, and the light and breeze that blows through the canyon is incredibly calming. She, too, as a person, is calming and has the ability to allow spaciousness in our conversations. Not every moment needs to be filled with words or questions. We sit in her backyard, coffee in hand, and watch hawks dip in and out of the trees, listen to the chirp of a hummingbird or the sound of a dog barking down the street. We listen to leaves rustling on the patio, the sound of her husband practicing piano, her kids chasing their friends inside the house. It's not an absence of sound, not all idyllic—but it is a break from us making sounds, taking time to listen to the sounds of life around us.

This kind of attentive presence where we spend time with nature without needing to do or accomplish anything is at the heart of the Japanese practice of *shinrin-yoku*, or forest bathing. Forest bathing is not about distance covered or trail conquered; it's about immersion, slowness, and simply noticing. When this practice became popular in the '80s in Japan, it had two primary purposes: first, to offer an "antidote to tech-boom burnout" and second, to help protect the forests.

Forest bathing falls under a broader umbrella of what's called *ecotherapy*, using nature to help improve both mental and physical health. Plenty of research ties the awe of nature to creativity and well-being. A study done through the University of California, Berkeley in 2016 showed that awe, often triggered by nature, expands our perception of time, increases generosity, and enhances well-being. The study also found a connection between awe and pattern recognition—a key to creative thinking.

Research shows that time in nature doesn't just calm our nervous system, it sharpens our attention, opens our thinking, and helps us connect to ideas in new ways.

You don't have to spend a night camping. You don't even need to be in a friend's yard. Connecting with nature can be as easy as visiting a park that has green in it, walking around the block, or looking out the window at a tree.

But the time outside needs to be distraction-free. This means you're not on a phone call or listening to a podcast, audiobook, or even music. To create the space you want in the walk, you want to limit distractions, not unlike a walking meditation.

Sometimes people push back on this, especially for longer walks. Take your device if you feel you need it to be safe or to count your steps. What I'm suggesting is that you don't use it. If you are walking to create spaciousness, being device-free makes sense. You're not going to create space by adding more inputs.

Spending time in nature offers the kind of spaciousness we can't manufacture with apps or planners. It invites our minds to lift, stretch, and reconnect with something larger than ourselves.

You don't need to climb a mountain or sleep under the stars. The simple act of stepping outside, without distraction but with attention, is enough to open the door to spaciousness and the potential of inspiration beyond.

EXERCISES

For You: Your Nature Connection Practice

1. **The Outdoor Audit:** Reflect on your last month—when did you spend undistracted time outside (no phone, podcast, or agenda)? Rate how that time affected your mental clarity and creative thinking. What patterns do you notice?

2. **The Ten-Minute Nature Experiment:** Identify one outdoor space within five minutes of your work or home. This week, spend ten minutes there without devices, three different times. Notice: What do you hear, see, smell? How does your thinking shift from when you arrived to when you leave?

For Your Team: Natural Meeting Innovation

1. **Walking Meeting Trial:** Choose one recurring team meeting and move it outside for a month. Track the difference in discussion quality, problem-solving, and team energy compared to indoor meetings. What types of conversations work best while walking?

   Strategy in the Fresh Air: Hold your next big-picture planning session outdoors for at least the first thirty minutes. Compare the breadth and creativity of ideas generated outside versus similar indoor sessions. How does the natural environment affect your team's strategic thinking?

20

BRING THE OUTSIDE IN

What happens when nature's not convenient, accessible, or visible? Maybe you're in a small apartment, on an airplane, or in a windowless office or overlooking cubicles or more offices? When you can't access nature, what are your options? How can you bring some of the outside in? The answer depends on the medium that works best for you—is it a video or images? Words on a page? Sounds?

During the pandemic, houseplant sales grew 18 percent as people attempted to bring the outside in. In the UK, the numbers were even higher. Lockdown conditions saw the sales of plants and bulbs rise nearly 3,000 percent at certain retailers. People filled their spaces with plants as a way to access nature when our geographic circles were constricted. The greenery and lushness made us feel like we could bring a little bit of what we were missing from the outside. And tending to those new plants helped to bring us mental spaciousness: Seventy-three percent of new plant buyers said caring for houseplants helped them cope with stress during the pandemic.

Why? The biophilia hypotheses is a concept that humans have an innate affinity for the natural world. Research shows that even small doses of nature, whether a houseplant or even a picture of a plant, can lower stress, sharpen focus, and support cognitive restoration. Cognitive restoration is like stoking the embers of the mind, letting fresh air flow in so focus and creativity can catch fire again. Bringing nature in isn't just about beauty; it's about giving our minds the space to breathe.

If a houseplant feels like too much of a commitment, a bouquet of flowers or a vase of tulips, especially in the clean light of morning or long lazy sun beams of afternoon, can connect us with nature.

Maybe plants and flowers aren't for you and your thumb just won't turn green. Incorporating natural material into your space, whether wood, wool, stone, or even rattan can help your surroundings feel more like nature. Nature can show up in the furniture, in the décor, or in small objects, like a bowl of pinecones or a collection of smooth river stones.

Another option is art. Finding photographs, paintings, or art of any kind that represents landscapes that resonate with you can also be an effective way to bring nature into your environment. Whether it's mountains or forest, beach or desert that speaks to you, finding an artistic representation that brings you joy can be a small way to bring that feeling of spaciousness to your indoor surroundings.

You can also choose to read about nature. Detailed, sensory-laden poetry about nature can be a good approximation of presence. Reading about nature can help bring the outside in—especially books that offer soothing, detailed, natural settings rather than ones focused on environmental disasters or high-stakes conservation efforts (at least not if you're looking for some mental spaciousness). There are many meditative books of nonfiction about nature (like Torbjorn Ekelund's work). Imagining yourself in those settings can bring about that same sense of space.

Headphones can be magical if you cannot find visual spaciousness in your home or office, or you're stuck on an airplane. When you can't create a sense of spaciousness physically or visually, try using music or sound. Over-the-ear headphones are great, but earbuds also work. We're not looking to do our best internal karaoke of our favorite songs—we want to create space. Any music with lyrics in a language we speak or understand can potentially distract us. Try creating space by listening to music without lyrics in whatever genre helps you to become calm and focused. For some people, that's classical; for others, it's jazz. You can find focus-themed playlists for house music, folk music, or EDM. You can experiment with listening to music with binaural beats, a type of sound-wave therapy where two slightly different sound frequencies are played in each ear through headphones. Some people believe that different frequencies can help with anything from concentration to relaxation, from flow state to sleep state. It's not magic, and research is underway to determine how effective binaural beats may be, but they're another example of a sound or "music" you can use to create spaciousness. Or try nature sounds: rain falling, waves crashing, or birdsong.

Smell can play a part too. Natural scents in candles, essential oils, room sprays, or diffusers can bring the outside in, whether cedar or eucalyptus, citrus or lavender. Fresh herbs like a sprig of rosemary or sage can pull double duty, providing both visual and aromatic support.

Each of these enhancers creates small sensory reminders of spaciousness. Even in limited physical space, you're helping your mind remember the expansive, calming quality of the natural world. There's no right way to do it. The key is finding what invites spaciousness for you, what quiets the noise in your brain and helps you feel more open and at ease.

EXERCISES

For You: Creating Your Natural Space

1. **The Sensory Audit:** Walk through your primary workspace and identify which of your five senses currently connect you to nature (or could). Rate each sense 1–10 for "nature connection." Pick your lowest-scoring sense and make one specific change this week—add a plant for sight, nature sounds for hearing, essential oils for smell, natural textures for touch, or herbal tea for taste.

2. **The Ten-Minute Nature Reset:** Create your personal "nature emergency kit" for when you're stuck indoors or in windowless spaces. It might include noise-cancelling headphones with a nature soundscape playlist, a small collection of natural objects (e.g., stones, pinecones, shells), or photos that transport you to your favorite outdoor place. Test it daily for one week during stressful moments. What do you notice?

For Your Team: Collective Nature Integration

1. **The Team Biophilia Map:** Have each team member identify their most effective way to connect with nature during work (e.g., using plants, natural light, sounds, scents, textures). Create a shared map of what works for whom, then collectively audit your shared spaces. What small changes could benefit the whole team's mental spaciousness?

2. **The Fresh Air Protocol:** Establish team rituals incorporating natural elements into your work rhythm. This could be "windows open" meetings when weather permits, starting team calls with thirty seconds of nature sounds, or designating one person each week to "bring nature to work" where that team member brings in flowers, plants, or something green.

PART 4

STILLNESS

21

THE ART OF MENTAL STILLNESS

Have you ever been so involved in a reading or listening to a book, so deep in the story and the characters, that your stomach rumbles and you realize several hours have passed and you've forgotten to eat? Maybe you've been out on the basketball court, playing one pickup game after the next and are surprised to look up and see the sun in a much different place than when you started. You could be in the woodshed or the garden, on a stand-up paddle-board, or sitting on the back patio playing guitar, and time flies by.

Absorption is that feeling when you are so immersed in an activity or specific moment that everything else, including time, fades away. The world around you becomes so incredibly still that you aren't even aware of it.

Absorption is the second precursor state of being that can lead us to inspiration.

If absorption is the end state, stillness is how we get there. Not literal stillness. Mental stillness.

Similarly, if focus is an end state (I realize it can also be an activity, so stay with me here), then we achieve it through directed attention.

We have a tendency to mistake a focused state for absorption, but the two are quite different. Not only do they present differently, but we use them for distinct purposes.

A state of absorption feels effortless, and that's different from focus. When we're focused, we're directing our attention to a specific task. Focus requires effort. Once we've focused our attention, we may or may not have that feeling of deep immersion.

Both absorption and focus require presence. We have to be in the moment to best direct our attention. But again, the intensity and the intent of focus and absorption varies. With focus, we're narrowing our inputs to intentionally direct our attention. Focus is like a flashlight with a narrow beam, tight, precise, and aimed at one single point. Absorption is the opposite. Absorption is like sunlight streaming through a window. The light is diffuse and touches everything in the room. It's wide, warm, and enveloping, creating an immersive environment where everything is bathed in light.

Each state brings about distinct outcomes. Let's go back to the reading example to help distinguish between a state of focus and a state of absorption. Focus is like reading a textbook, studying each line, highlighting, taking notes. There's intention behind our attention and often a goal we want to achieve. In that way, our focus is deliberate. Absorption is just like the example at the opening of chapter—the experience of getting so lost in a story or characters that time melts away. It's a deeper and more immersive state that doesn't have any of the effort associated with focus. When we sit down to read and achieve a state of absorption, we don't have a goal or an intention. Focus is directed toward a mental destination whereas in absorption, we're just along for the ride.

When we focus, we are doing with the intent of doing. When we are in absorption, we are doing but with the intent of being.

Aside from different outcomes, absorption and focus reap different types of rewards. Focus often has an extrinsic reward. We may not reap that reward immediately, but focus moves us toward a specific achievement or goal that is visible and/or measurable. Absorption is more closely tied to an intrinsic reward. In a state of absorption, we may feel a sense of satisfaction, enjoyment, or even personal growth.

The downside? We tend to dismiss the intrinsic rewards and devalue those activities, regardless of the amount of peace or joy they may bring us. As a result, we are also far more likely to push them to the side. And there's the problem. Because we associate these activities with something intrinsic and therefore less important, we are less likely to give ourselves permission to engage in them. Whether we're working through a strategic plan that keeps evading us, or a reshuffle of talent at work, or a plan to support a family member or navigate a divorce, we shy away from stillness. But we're happy to allow ourselves focus time to put our head down and mentally muscle through it. The focus time may help, but when we're really stuck, our most creative and workable solutions come from the state of absorption. To get there, we need stillness.

How does absorption differ from "flow state"? Flow state is more a blend of focus and absorption. Focus, skill, and challenge are all present in that state of being. In this book, and in the service of getting us to an inspired state (which is also different from a flow state), we'll keep our attention on absorption.

In the following pages, I'll offer strategies for stillness rather than absorption. Why? Because I want to spend time on how you get to the state of absorption rather than the state itself.

By "stillness," I don't mean physical stillness but rather the stillness you get in your brain when you're so absorbed in an activity that the rest of the world falls away. But keep this in mind: "Stillness" and "doing" are not mutually exclusive or at odds. The key is how we define "doing." Are we focused on the destination or the journey?

In his book *Stillness Is the Key*, Ryan Holiday describes the role of stillness and its outcomes. "Stillness aims the archer's bow. It inspires new ideas. It sharpens perspective and illuminates connection."

Stillness goes hand in hand with spaciousness. When I first started writing this book, I described spaciousness, stillness, and self-forgetfulness as the legs of a stool that are most likely to support us in finding inspiration. And while that's partially true, as all three states in conjunction may lead to inspiration, they also build on one another. It's difficult to find stillness if you don't first have spaciousness, and it's difficult to experience the feeling of self-forgetfulness if you don't first have stillness.

As I've played with these concepts, I've come to realize they're closer to the rungs of a ladder or stair steps, each one building on the one before and bringing us closer to the elevation and height of inspiration. Spaciousness clears and sets the table, stillness happens once we sit down at the table to eat, and self-forgetfulness is the seasoning that makes the meal memorable.

The next few chapters offer tactics to help you create stillness so that you can ease into a ready state for inspiration.

Ready to discover where you stand with stillness? Before we explore the how-to's, let's take a moment to assess where you're starting from. This brief quiz will reveal your current relationship with this essential state.

QUIZ

1. **How often do you become so immersed or absorbed in something that time disappears?**
   a. Rarely—I'm usually aware of time passing and what's happening around me.
   b. Occasionally—maybe when I'm reading or doing a hobby I really love.
   c. Regularly—I can get absorbed in various activities throughout my week.
   d. I'm not sure I've ever experienced this feeling.

2. **What's your relationship with "doing nothing" or unstructured time?**
   a. I feel guilty or anxious, like I should always be productive or working toward a goal.
   b. I enjoy it but struggle to give myself permission to have it.
   c. I actively protect and value unstructured time as essential for my well-being.
   d. I fill every moment with activities; even "relaxing" ones must have a purpose.

3. **When you're stuck on a problem, your instinct is to:**
   a. Push harder and focus more intensely until I break through.
   b. Take a brief break but get back to focused work quickly.
   c. Step away completely and let my mind wander until insight comes.
   d. Alternate between intense focus and complete mental breaks.

4. **Which statement best describes your experience with activities you love?**
   a. I rarely make time for them—there's always something more important to do.
   b. I do them but often feel like I should be doing something more "productive".
   c. I lose myself in them completely, and time flies by without me noticing.
   d. I enjoy them, but my mind often wanders to work or other responsibilities.

5. **Your biggest challenge with finding stillness is:**
   a. I don't know how to quiet my mind—thoughts keep racing.
   b. I feel like stillness is a luxury I can't afford right now.
   c. I can find stillness but struggle to value it as much as focused work.
   d. I'm not even sure what stillness would feel like for me.

What your answers mean:

If you're mostly **A's or D's**, you're likely caught in the focus trap—believing that mental effort is always the answer. Start experimenting with activities that naturally draw you in without a goal attached.

If you're mostly **B's**, you understand the value of stillness but need permission to prioritize it. Practice reframing absorption activities as essential rather than optional.

If you're mostly **C's**, you're already tapping into stillness regularly. Focus on protecting these experiences and helping others understand their importance for your creativity and problem-solving.

22

DON'T FEAR THE VOID

One of the challenges we have around creating stillness is our desire to fill the void. The pace of modern life makes that easy to do.

For many people, a void conjures images of an oppressive and complete darkness, a nothingness that is both terrifying and complete. It's an inky dark ocean with who-knows-what lurking beneath the surface.

No wonder we try to fill "the void." A study conducted at University of California, San Francisco in 2014 found that people would rather shock themselves than be alone with their thoughts. Whether that's because of a discomfort with negative emotions, ego protection, or even some biological wiring, that's how much we try to avoid the void.

Even if our fear isn't quite that strong, we want to make sure we use every moment to be productive, to "keep up," to make movement. Previous chapters explored the need to make space, whether through time blocking or permission slips. On those Saturdays when we give ourselves permission to just be, to forget about following a timeline or a list of to-dos, we often have our greatest moments of clarity.

My friend Jen recently told me about her Saturday. She'd planned a day crammed with errands, including grocery shopping, house cleaning, dog training class, swimming, and a Zoom call with a friend overseas.

She woke up that morning anxious, wondering how she'd weave through everything like gates on a giant slalom run. She said she felt like if she missed one gate, she'd mess up her entire day. Her anxiety didn't just stem from finishing tasks; it was the mental gymnastics of figuring out the order and timing, and whether or not she could get it all done. She knew she could expect a constant murmur of "I need to's" and "What's next's" pinging around in her mind all day.

So she took a step back and sorted her mental list into what was absolutely necessary and what was on her wish list. Much to her surprise, not one thing on that list was absolutely necessary for her to complete that day. Her brain was pressuring her to do it all, but once she listened to her body, she gave herself permission to choose what she wanted to do. She narrowed the list to just four things that felt the most fulfilling.

As our day stretches, our minds do, too, standing on tiptoe with their fingers in the air. This feels marvelous. What does your most relaxing day look and feel like? Create a portrait in detail and ask yourself how you can incorporate just a few more moments of stillness every day.

This is the type of spaciousness and stillness we need to invite inspiration.

We often fill our own voids, even on a Saturday in early summer, when we could be slowing down and enjoying our lives. For some of us, this drive to complete or engage in activities that keep us busy is almost compulsive. We can trick ourselves into thinking an activity may be pleasurable, specifically anything that's screen-based. We could be researching ideas for the next dream house project, shopping for clothes, scrolling on social media, or playing a game on our phone. In small doses, these are all okay. But these activities don't create mental stillness in most people. Several studies show the correlation between smartphone use and increased stress and emotional dysregulation (the inability to control emotions). When we use our phone to fill in the spaciousness time we've set aside for ourselves, we're not getting the benefit of stillness. Screen time allows for the low hum of mental chatter to continue in our brains.

Stillness isn't the absence of doing; it's the presence of being. When we stop trying to fill every gap with a different level of noise, we can create a space where inspiration can find us.

EXERCISES

For You: The Void Audit

1. **Track Your Gap-Fillers:** For three days, notice what you automatically reach for during quiet moments, like grabbing your phone, doing tasks, or engaging in planning. Simply observe without judgment. What patterns emerge?

2. **The Unstructured Hour:** Block one hour this week with zero agenda. No goals, no productivity, no "should dos." If anxiety arises about "wasting time," sit with that feeling. What comes up when you're not filling the space?

For Your Team: Collective Stillness Practice

1. **Meeting Silence Bookends:** Start meetings with sixty seconds of silent preparation (no devices, just breathing and arriving mentally) and end with thirty seconds of silent transition time before people rush off to their next commitment.

   The Single-Task Challenge: Have each team member choose one routine task they normally multitask while doing (emails, calls, planning) and commit to doing it solo for one week. Share observations about focus, quality, and mental state differences.

23

DIGITAL QUICKSAND
AND OTHER TRAPS

I had been working with my client Peter to create spaciousness and time for stillness to figure out his next steps to prepare for the sale of his company. Not just the nuts and bolts around financials and reporting and data rooms but who he wanted to be in the next chapter of life.

Peter committed to setting aside the time and a place to sit in stillness. He chose a park on his daily commute between his home and office.

In our next meeting, I asked him how it went.

"Not well, D, not well."

"Oh no! What happened?"

"Well, I got to the park, and I was ready to go. I got out of the car, walked to this lovely bench underneath a tree, and just as I sat down, I got a message on Slack. I knew it was only going to take me a second to respond, so I did. A few client emails had come in during my drive over, so I responded to those. And then I was good. I got settled into the bench, put my phone away, and was just looking around. I was watching some guys getting ready to play pickleball, and it reminded me that I wanted to set up time with some friends to play, so I sent out a group text. Then we started talking about the Padres on the text thread, and before you know it, all my stillness time was gone, and I had to get to a meeting."

Does his experience seem familiar to you?

Peter's experience reveals a common trap. Even when we create space to be still, things still pop up. When you eliminate distractions, you can spread your thoughts out like they're on a giant piece of paper. But when distraction kicks in, that paper gets shredded into tiny pieces and tossed in the air like confetti. Confetti is fun, for sure, but doesn't help your stillness.

In theory, there shouldn't be that many distractions, right? You've taken care of them by clearing your calendar, setting boundaries, potentially even finding a physical space that allows you this time to sink into stillness. Hey, you even drove to the park! How many distractions could there be? Oh, but there are still so many. Especially depending on when and where you've created this time. The challenge isn't only external interruptions but also the self-imposed ones.

If you're near a device of any kind—laptop, tablet, phone— then the challenge can be the apps, the games, the internet. Isn't it easier for you to check the standings of your favorite team than to sit in stillness? Play one more round of Two Dots? Check whatever form of social media you love most? Maybe distraction even masks itself in productivity. You tell yourself, "I just need to check email really quickly," or "Let me finish this presentation," or "I want to take a peek at where we are against month-to-date on our revenue goals."

You trick yourself into thinking you're just taking a quick side quest, like Peter did. But just like the 1970s and '80s when we were all worried about quicksand, these small tasks or "quick checks" are mental quicksand. You fall into them without knowing, unaware that your time is draining away as you sink into the task, only to realize you are up to your neck in this side quest without having spent a moment in stillness time.

How do you protect yourself from these digital demons? Start with your devices. If you need to have it on, shut down all applications except what you absolutely need. Better? Put every device on airplane mode or Do Not Disturb. Better yet? Put all other devices in another room. Best case, power off anything you're not using.

Many of us have a love/hate relationship with our phones but feel dependent on them for both personal and professional reasons. We connect with friends, family, and clients, use them to book dinner reservations or classes at the gym, even to refill our prescriptions. The list of productive uses for our phones is endless.

And yet, many times we can feel like we'd love nothing more than to huck it into the ocean or any other abyss. The phone can feel like it demands so much of us. It's also a huge distraction. Why yes, I *would* love to watch another video of a dog with a voice-over, and yes, I find that little girl who put on her mother's lipstick adorable. Because the videos are so short, we feel like we have the time to watch just one more. But there's always just one more after that, and after that one, and after that one.

Turning devices completely off, rather than Do Not Disturb, closes the figurative door on digital distractions completely. When your phone is on, even in Do Not Disturb mode, it keeps the door of your accessibility cracked open, undermining your boundaries.

In addition to helping curb the distraction, there's a peacefulness that comes from having devices off. We're constantly available, and we've come to expect that from one another. Years ago, Baby Boomers experienced the luxury of being out of touch once they left the office. On vacation, unless someone called the hotel directly or knew the phone number of the place where they were staying, there was no way to get a hold of them. They could be unreachable for hours or days. Later generations never knew that feeling.

It can feel scary to turn our devices off. "What if someone needs me?" Most things can wait. Truly. This goes back to our Eisenhower matrix exercise from the Ruthless Prioritization chapter. If there is an emergency, those around you still have their devices on, or someone can show up at your door like we used to do a few decades ago.

So rest easy and turn that damn thing off.

Let's say it's a crazy day. Your brain is sparking all over the place, and you're not making any headway with stillness where a device is involved. I get it. Ideally, we're not on devices at all during stillness time (but not focus time). Try taking that idea for a presentation out of the office and to the bench outside with a notebook and some pens—maybe even colored pencils. Maybe you choose to work through next year's budget on an abacus. I kid. What if you spent time thinking about the type of organization or department you wanted to be first, before you built your budget? What if you took the time to figure out what was important, what your clients or vendors or competitors would say about you, and then you drew that out in images? These are great examples of stillness time well spent.

One last thing about external distractions. Especially if we're prone to distraction because of ADHD or any other reason, it can be easy to revert to judging ourselves. We might even abandon the stillness time because it's "too hard" or we "can't focus." We'll talk more in the next section about our own internal distractions and of the various ways that you can engage in stillness, whether you're physically still or not.

EXERCISES

For You: The Distraction Defense System

1. **Map Your Mental Quicksand:** List your top five distraction triggers during quiet moments (e.g., phone notifications, email alerts, mental to-do lists, nearby devices). Rate each 1–10 for how often it derails your stillness attempts.

2. **The Twenty-Minute Fortress:** Create one completely distraction-free zone for twenty minutes this week. Turn devices completely off (not just silenced), remove visual triggers, and sit with whatever comes up. Note: The goal isn't perfect stillness; it's practicing non-reaction to distractions.

For Your Team: Collective Boundary Setting

1. **Team Distraction Inventory:** Have everyone anonymously share their top three workplace distractions. Create a team map of shared distraction patterns and collectively choose one to address (like notification-free focus blocks or device-free meeting periods).

2. **The Unreachable Experiment:** Challenge the team to establish one hour per week when everyone is simultaneously "unreachable"—no Slack, email, or instant responses. Start small and track what happens during these protected periods compared to fears about what might happen.

24

QUIETING THE JUDGE

Let's assume we've done a great job setting time aside for stillness, we've eliminated the external distractions, and we're finally sitting down (or getting up) to be still. Even in moments of quiet or those in which we may be engaged in our favorite hobby, sometimes our Judge slips in quietly through the back door.

Who's our Judge? It's the voice in our heads that's wildly critical of everything. Our inner Judges have a tendency to kick us in the shins no matter the topic. They comment on the big stuff, such as our leadership (e.g., "You're a terrible leader. That was the worst decision ever. Why did you ever think you'd be good at this?"), or something little, like when we're on a bike ride around the neighborhood ("Look at you huffing and puffing up this small hill. Look who's out of shape! I'll bet people driving by are laughing at you.").

When our Judge is present, the stillness we normally achieve when we're writing or knitting, rowing or sowing, biking or hiking, is interrupted. Whether we're doing our favorite thing as stress release, as part of our stillness practice, or just for fun, the Judge can rain on the parade. Stillness creates a vacuum, and the Judge rushes to fill it. We're so used to background noise, whether it consists of tasks, conversations, or distractions, that in the quiet, the Judge's voice can be deafening.

That's normal.

The Judge isn't just annoying; it also crowds out the mental spaciousness where inspiration happens. When the Judge is loud, we react by protecting ourselves, not focusing on possibility, curiosity, or creation.

The Judge can be sneaky. Sometimes it masks its voice in logic, and this makes it harder to identify. Let me give you an example.

I was working on a gift for a very close friend celebrating a milestone birthday. I love to craft, something I inherited from a long line of crafters on my mother's side. One of my most prized possessions is a jewelry box my mother made for me from chipboard and matchboxes covered in Chiyogami paper. I love the little details of it—the tiny drawers with brads for knobs, the beautiful paper, the wooden beads for feet. It's creative, fun, and delightful. When my mom passed away, one of the small joys of cleaning out her craft room was finding the instructions on how to make this jewelry box.

The project itself wasn't terribly complicated but had quite a few steps. When I first started, I was a little nervous because I hadn't ever made this jewelry box before. But I was also very excited. I gathered all the materials and started cutting paper and prepping. Everything was going along fabulously until I started painting the bottom of the matchboxes that serve as the drawers of the jewelry box. The paint kept streaking, and the brads I was using for drawer pulls weren't perfectly centered. I kept thinking about how my mother would have made a better version. How my friend would be disappointed if she took out one of the matchbox drawers, flipped it over, and saw that the paint was a bit streaky. I was embarrassed that the final product might look messy and unprofessional. I wondered what my friend might think about me or what I thought of our relationship, that she might perceive that I was careless or sloppy, that I hadn't put enough effort in to make it perfect.

As I moved on to cutting the chipboard, I noticed my anxiety spiking. All of a sudden it struck me that the process of making this gift, which had meant so much to me and was really something pretty cool that my friend would absolutely adore, had turned from fun and relaxing to stressful and anxiety-provoking. All because my type A, overachieving, high-need-for-perfection personality traits, and my Judge, had hijacked my brain. I imagined my Judge like an umpire in a tennis match, sitting high up in her chair, commenting on every little thing that I did. Except she's not the least bit fair and can be incredibly cruel.

I was shocked. I hadn't even realized that my Judge had shown up. To quiet her, I reminded myself that (a) this was supposed to be fun, (b) the stakes were not high here—this was a gift for a friend who would adore it, no matter what, and (c) however the box turned out would be perfect. It truly was the thought that counted. It also reminded me of how stealthily Judges can creep into the most benign situations. We can be in the middle of something pretty amazing, and it's like they sneak in with Groucho Marx glasses and crash the party.

When we're trying to get still, whether through activity or just sitting, what do we do when the Judge shows up?

The most important step is to recognize the Judge's voice in our minds. It can be hard for many of us to hear, because we've lived with that little voice for the majority of our lives, regardless of how and when it started. One way to recognize that voice is to run those thoughts through what I call the "friend filter." Go back to the words in your brain and ask yourself, "Would I say those words to my best friend? To my sister? To someone I care deeply about?" If your response is a horrified "No, of course not!" you can be pretty sure what you've been hearing is your Judge talking loud and proud, squawking at you from that high tennis chair.

Another way to recognize the Judge is to pay attention to your mood when engaging in an activity and noticing how your body is reacting. When anxiety shows, it normally has a physical calling card. It might be a distinct tightening of your solar plexus or a stomachache. Some people notice a tightness in their chest, or maybe their heart rate picks up. Still others get a headache when they are anxious or nervous. I've got a friend whose shoulders bunch up and tighten. Using our bodies as our barometer can be another way to recognize that the Judge has snuck into our brains.

In his book *The War of Art*, Steven Pressfield calls this voice "Resistance." Resistance is the force that stymies our creative juices and blocks us through fear, self-doubt, and procrastination. It often pops up in moments of stillness and when we try to do something creative and new. When we're super busy, we may be less conscious of it, but when we've finally made the spaciousness for ourselves, and are just sitting down (or getting up) to stillness, we'll hear it creep in.

Regardless of how it got there, now that the Judge is solidly on our radar, we need to get it to pipe down, or as I lovingly tell my own Judge, "Shut your pie hole." Depending on the level of anxiety or imposter syndrome you're feeling, you may need to be more or less direct. If your Judge is really on a tirade, the easiest way to get them to back off is *not* to directly challenge them or even ask, "What's true here?" The Judge will tell you that all the worst things are true with every piece of evidence they can gather and throw it all in your face.

Instead, you could ask, "What's more helpful to believe?" because this isn't something that can necessarily be argued. As an example, you can be out in the garden quietly weeding, and the Judge can chime in, "You should know more about this by now. That plant's probably going to die." Maybe that's true. You *could* know more about gardening, and yeah, that plant isn't looking so great. But the response isn't helpful. You can instead ask yourself what's more helpful to believe. Maybe it would be that you could learn more about gardening, although you know a lot already.

This plant may not look great, but the rest of the garden does. This may be your first attempt at growing passion fruit, so you may need to show yourself grace or patience as you learn how to best tend to it.

Another way to quiet the Judge is to say, "Maybe later." Just like you tell your nieces who want to go out for ice cream, your partner who wants to watch a show while you're trying to finish something, the colleague who wants to grab coffee while you're buried in work. If you can just put your hand up and tell that Judge you're willing to listen to anything they say but "Not now, maybe later," it can help to shut them down.

Some people give their Judge a ridiculous name. We've all heard of Negative Nancy, but what about Queen Nitpickia? Buzz-kill Bill? The Shouldinator?

Others use mantras when their Judge shows up: "I choose stillness over judgment," or "Thanks for your opinion, I'm good," or maybe, "I'm allowed to enjoy this."

One method of last resort is to grin and bear it. If the Judge is really going off, just keep on doing what you're doing. Maybe you're out for a run, finally on a peaceful path, breathing in fresh air, and despite your Judge jawing about the fact that you're so slow, just got passed, and should go home, you keep running. Sometimes the Judge will quiet because their words aren't stopping you from doing what you want to do. They storm off, pouting, maybe shouting an obscenity or two over their shoulders while slinking back into the shadows of your mind.

Don't panic if you sit down to stillness and the Judge shows up. They will visit because that's part of being human. The magic of stillness is that with practice, we can notice the Judge's voice, smile at it, and then return to what matters. Quieting the Judge isn't about silencing every inner critic forever. It's about creating just enough peace for inspiration to come through—loud and clear.

EXERCISES

For You: The Judge Detection System

1. **Physical Early Warning Signs:** Identify your body's specific signals when the Judge arrives (e.g., tight shoulders, stomach knots, racing heart). Practice a thirty-second body scan during stillness activities to catch the Judge before they fully take over.

2. **The Friend Filter Practice:** When you catch judgmental thoughts during stillness time, immediately ask: "Would I say this to my best friend?" If the answer is no, respond with a compassionate reframe: "I'm learning," or "This is enough," or "I'm exactly where I need to be."

For Your Team: Creating Judge-Free Zones

1. **The Perfectionism Audit:** In your next team meeting, have everyone write down one work activity where their inner Judge is loudest (e.g., presentations, client calls, creative work). Identify patterns and normalize the experience—most people will discover they're not alone in their self-criticism.

2. **Practice Rounds Protocol:** For high-stakes activities where the Judge typically shows up (e.g., big presentations, difficult conversations), create "practice rounds" where the explicit goal is experimentation, not perfection. Debrief what people noticed about their internal dialogue when the pressure to be perfect is removed.

25

MEDITATION 101

We've created the spaciousness we need, resisted the temptation to fill the void, and eliminated both external and internal distractions like the Judge, so now what?

It's a valid question. We're not used to having time to be still, so it makes sense that we may not know what to do with time when we have it.

Stillness, in its purest form, is agenda- and focus-free. We engage in stillness to quiet our minds enough so that we can set them free. Stillness isn't just a pause; it's the soil in which ideas germinate.

Please forgive me for this, but the simplest form of stillness is being still. It seems like that's obvious, but it's a surprise to some people. You can practice traditional forms of meditation, guided or unguided. It doesn't matter if you've been meditating for years or you're starting today. Some meditation has us pay attention to our breath, our inhales and exhales, the feel of air in our nostrils or the sound of our breath leaving our lungs. Meditation can be watching the steam rise from a hot cup of tea or spending time looking out a window or watching clouds drift across the sky. It can also be people-watching or gazing at dogs, squirrels, and birds. We can meditate at home, in the office, or even in our car.

Listening is a wonderful way to enjoy stillness. We can listen to music, to the ticking of a clock, or to rain pattering on a rooftop, sounds we normally associate with peace and stillness. But we don't need babbling brooks, the sound of ocean waves, or harp music to be present. We just need to listen, in every detail, to what's going on around us. We might hear an AC unit rattling, a dog barking, a saw buzzing, a baby fussing, someone talking on the phone, or the bass bumping in a car as it passes. We are just listening, not to hear anything in particular, not to be a certain way, but simply to listen. We are listening for listening's sake.

We can engage our sense of touch, noticing our feet in our shoes or feeling them on the floor. We can notice the sensation of sitting, on our sit bones, thighs resting against the cushion, back leaning against the chair.

Whether you're watching, listening, or feeling, pay close attention to your thoughts. The stillness is meant to slow and smooth the ripples of thought as much as possible so that we can start to loosely think about whatever we need help with.

It's common to have trouble getting those ripples to still while we're meditating. My sister shared this Buddhist way of looking at thoughts. Think of standing on a small wooden bridge over a rushing stream, where your thoughts are like leaves on the surface. Your job is just to notice the leaves and watch them slip by. The perspective shift from "in the river" to "over the river" can help us gain distance from those thoughts. Sometimes a great idea will sneak in like a bright orange leaf on a gurgling stream.

Your mind will wander. It always does. That's not failure; it's the process.

I want to be clear, and most meditation teachers will tell you, the point of meditation is not necessarily to clear our thoughts but to be aware of them. It's one of the reasons stillness can be harder to maintain or achieve in meditation for those less practiced. But I'm a firm believer that no matter how fast your mind goes, meditation can help you achieve stillness.

Years ago, I was going through a period of great change, and my anxiety began to spike. Regardless of the spaciousness or stillness I carved out of my day to try to refocus and ground myself, I couldn't tame my anxiety. I tried several different coping techniques, but none of them felt sustainable. Someone recommended I take a mindfulness meditation class. I'd dabbled in meditation previously but never committed to a practice. Part of the reason I lacked commitment was because I always felt like I was doing it "wrong."

This fear of doing it wrong happens often with new meditators, but I didn't know that at the time. Over the course of a few weeks while I waffled about signing up for the class, I finally got to the point where my anxiety had wrestled my perfectionism to the ground and pinned it there. I knew I needed new skills and a larger toolset to work through my anxiety, so I signed up for the program.

The class was a game changer for me. Yes, the class taught me about meditation and that almost any way you engage in meditation is *the right way*. I learned different forms of meditation, but the kind that stayed with me the longest and had the most profound impact was walking meditation. In walking meditation, you move very slowly and deliberately, ideally outside, and notice everything.

I remember the first time we did a walking meditation on a late Saturday morning in early spring. The air outside was crisp and the sky a delicate blue, and the sun in that time of year has a gentler light to it. Our teacher rang the bell as I stood in front of a wall covered in brilliant pink bougainvillea. I noticed the curve of each petal, the small star-like pistil in each bloom, an ant crawling across one of the flowers. The way the bright pink stood out against the light blue of the morning sky. The curve of the vines against the wall. There was so much life, activity, and beauty in such a small space. I remember coming back into the room afterward and telling our teacher how if I paid that close attention on a walk, I'd likely never get further than my own block. It allowed me to so completely still my thoughts, I was almost incredulous.

Walking meditation (or meditation of any kind) is another way that you can practice being still. Choose a place for your walking meditation where you feel safe and calm, free from overwhelming distractions, so your mind can rest lightly on something simple like a tree branch or a windowsill. It works when your mind is already relatively still, or conversely, when it is careening wildly out of control.

If meditation is not your jam but prayer is, consider prayer as just another form of meditation—it can provide similar benefits. Many religions have certain prayers that are recited repeatedly. In Catholicism, some people find great stillness in praying the rosary, which is a series of more than fifty prayers. Reciting the same lines over and over can bring about peaceful stillness.

Stillness isn't about emptying your mind; it's about creating space for what matters. It's where presence becomes possible and fresh ideas can find a foothold. You don't need to sit for hours or do it "perfectly." Even a few mindful breaths, a deliberate walk, or a short time to sit and listen can recalibrate your attention and create a pause where inspiration can get through the traffic in your brain.

If you feel that "Meditation isn't for me. I can't get my brain that still," consider that anything gets easier with practice. When the pinwheels in our brains are spinning out of control, finding a way to still them can feel difficult regardless of whether we're in traditional meditation or walking meditation. But the effort is worth it. The next chapter will explore a few other ways to engage in stillness.

EXERCISES

For You: Your Stillness Starter Kit

1. **The Five-Minute Experiment:** Try three different stillness approaches this week (e.g., traditional sitting meditation, walking meditation, mindful listening). Spend five minutes with each and note which feels most natural. There's no wrong choice—you're building your personal stillness portfolio.

2. **The Ripple Watch:** During any stillness practice, when thoughts arise, practice the "bridge over the stream" technique. Simply notice each thought like it's a leaf floating by without trying to grab it. After the exercise, track how many "leaves" passed in five minutes. Do they slow down over time?

For Your Team: Stillness Integration

1. **Meeting Meditation Trial:** Introduce sixty seconds of silent presence at the start of three consecutive team meetings. Frame it as "arriving in the room together." After the trial, gather honest feedback: What did people notice about their focus and presence, and the quality of the meeting?

2. **The Wandering Mind Normalize:** In your next team check-in, ask everyone to share their biggest distraction during focused work time. Then explain that meditation research shows that the wandering mind is normal—noticing and returning builds the skill. This reassures team members who think they're "bad" at stillness.

26

STILLNESS IN MOTION

Not everyone finds stillness in the traditional sense. Some of us find peace not in quietude but in rhythm. Our minds slow down when our bodies speed up in familiar patterns. Let's look at stillness that moves.

Stillness that moves includes activities that have repetitive motion, that you're familiar with (vs. learning something new that's going to require a lot of focus or attention), and that you can do almost in autopilot. Your muscles know what to do and your thoughts can wander freely. Stillness in motion is still stillness, and it counts.

You may find mental stillness in outdoor movement, in the sound of your snowboard cutting across a mountain run or the burn of your quads as you bike up a steep hill. You may feel it as you sit on the rocks at the beach or in the quiet of your backyard. Stillness might find you hitting one golf ball after the next at the driving range or dribbling and making layup after layup in the driveway. You could be lifting weights in your garage or dipping your kayak paddle in and out of the water.

Stillness comes from indoor rhythms, too, like the way your spoon stirs a bubbling pot of sauce or your hands knead dough. You may be singing or dancing, banging on drums or strumming a guitar. You could be woodworking or jewelry-making, glassblowing or diamond-painting. Maybe you're working on the edges of a jigsaw puzzle or pruning back honeysuckle. You could be stretching into a downward dog in yoga or have your feet in straps on a Pilates reformer. Some of these "active stillness" hobbies can even be carried into the office, like knitting or whittling, puzzles or drawing during breaks.

Sometimes active stillness is as simple as sensory grounding, like rubbing your dog's ears or feeling the rumble of your cat purring on your lap.

A number of clients find stillness in cleaning. Some love to wipe down a counter and others to run a vacuum.

Active stillness could even be something as simple as organizing.

When I was little, my mom's nanny, Lucy, had a great big jar of buttons. She'd spill them out on the table and let us play with them and organize them however we wanted, based on shape or size or color. There was something very meditative but playful in this for me. I created row upon row of different types of buttons, pushing them into the center when I was done, and starting all over. And while I sorted these buttons, I could make up all kinds of stories and fairy tales, using the buttons in make-believe. The activity allowed me to be slightly physically and mentally active while giving my brain the space to be creative. You can do this with anything: sea glass or shells, beads or buttons, Legos or loose change. You can keep a jar of these items on your desk to quickly and relatively neatly drop into stillness.

Regardless of which activity helps you find mental stillness, you need to be able to do it and still hum. Weird requirement, right? If you can hum, a few things are happening (or not happening). First, you have enough mental space (what we're going for here) to be able to do two things at once. A study published in January 2024 suggested that low-frequency noise, like humming, can negatively impact higher-order cognitive functioning and reasoning. So if you're working on mathematical calculations, data processing, or logical reasoning, low-frequency noise may interrupt it. This is a good warning sign for us. Here's Danielle's humming rule: If you can't hum while doing the hobby you're engaged in, it's taking up too much cognitive bandwidth to allow your mind to drift.

Any of these activities that allow us to hum will fit the bill when it comes to stillness and giving ourselves mental spaciousness in addition to physical spaciousness. You don't need to do the same thing every day. One day you may sit and study the details of a picture on the wall and the next day pull weeds for twenty minutes.

Stillness doesn't always look like a still glass of water. Sometimes it hums, or kneads dough, or skates. Maybe it sings along. The key is consistency. The more you allow yourself the stillness, the more likely it is that inspiration will appear.

EXERCISES:

For You: Building Your Stillness Menu

1. **The Humming Test:** Try three different activities this week that you think might create stillness for you. During each one, try to hum. If you can hum comfortably while doing the activity, it passes the test for mental spaciousness. Create your personal "stillness menu" from these activities.

2. **The Fifteen-Minute Commitment:** From your stillness menu, pick one activity and commit to fifteen minutes of it within the next three days. No goals, no improvement focus, no multitasking—just the activity itself. Notice what thoughts or insights bubble up during or afterward.

For Your Team: Workplace Stillness Discovery

1. **The Office-Friendly Audit:** Have team members brainstorm stillness activities that could work in or near the workplace (e.g., walking meetings, desk organizing, doodling during calls, brief outdoor breaks). Create a shared list of "office-appropriate stillness" options.

2. **The Midday Reset Experiment:** Challenge your team to try one ten-minute stillness-in-motion activity (e.g., walking, stretching, organizing, even mindful coffee making) during their workday for one week. Share observations: Did it impact focus, creativity, or problem-solving?

27

IMAGINATION AS INSPIRATION FUEL

When we were kids, anything was possible, and our imaginations raced across the sky like a kite in the wind. Do you remember how much you used your imagination? For most of us, it ran wild.

What do you think of when someone says the word *imagination* now? Often when asked to use our imagination as adults, we automatically scoff at the request. It can feel infantile, patronizing, or like a waste of time. We may correlate imagination with make-believe or with the impossible, and as a result, we often dismiss it out of hand.

Imagination isn't just for kids and screenwriters. Imagination and big-picture thinking can come just before or just after a strike of inspiration.

Imagination at its root calls on creativity, curiosity, and wonder and can be applied to anything from dragons and unicorns to solving cash-flow problems (though using your imagination toward cash flow is probably not nearly as fun).

Imagination is also the perfect state to get us to inspiration. That same open-chested, light feeling we get when we're inspired also shows up when we use our imagination. We can use our imagination to think about everything that could go wrong, like worst-case scenarios, darkness, and disaster—but the imagination we're talking about here is the positive kind.

There is so much science around visualization and its impact on our ability to achieve our goals. Vivid mental simulations activate the same brain regions used in memory, problem-solving, emotion, and motivation. Imagining ideal outcomes increases our confidence and willingness to pursue them, especially when we do so with consistency and frequency. The outcomes of imagination are real and relevant, especially related to creating the stillness needed for inspiration to arrive.

At work, imagination can help us envision new products, strategies, or possibilities. When we deliberately harness imagination during stillness, we can surface creative solutions that evade logical analysis. We can strengthen commitment to goals by rehearsing success. The capacity for divergent thinking also improves when we use our imagination, as we're more able to link ideas across contexts.

Imagination can give us greater perspective, getting over the humps or challenges that seem insurmountable. It gets us closer to our why, to our purpose, to building a life, a dream, an organization, or a community we've only dreamed possible. When we apply imagination, what seemed impossible becomes possible.

And it's the perfect use of some of our stillness time.

We're now clear about the power and relevance of imagination, right? The question then is how to harness and nourish it. Here are a few ways we can play with imagination during our stillness time.

What-If Scenarios

When we start mapping out the "what-ifs," most people go straight to the worst-case, what I call "van down by the river" scenarios. But what if you imagined the best outcomes? What if you imagined the presentation going so well next week that the investor wrote a check on the spot? What if the conversation with a contentious peer at work went so well that you were able to build a failsafe process between your departments that increased efficiency by 50 percent? What if you were able to run that sub-eight-minute mile during your upcoming race?

This powerful exercise ties stillness to inspiration. If we allow ourselves to believe, to think about what happens if everything turns out just like we'd want, or maybe better, we can see even wider horizons.

Reframe the Mundane

Sometimes we get stuck in a line of thinking. One way to break out of that is to use our imagination on everyday objects and think about alternative uses. Start with something in your line of sight. What are the alternative uses for a coffee mug? It could hold pens or pencils or be a cute plant holder. You can use it as a soup or cereal bowl. Maybe you use it as a lamp base or part of a trophy you build for your team. You could decorate the inside of it and make it into a diorama or a gratitude jar, a container where you drop notes of gratitude. If you really amp up your imagination, maybe that mug is magical and gives you the power to be invisible . . . or it's the portal to another dimension. The more creative you are, the better. Even if you can't use this same line of thinking for something you may be working on or struggling with, it's a great way to tap into your creativity and nonlinear thinking.

Creative Constraints

Have you ever tried writing a poem? It could be a "Roses are red, violets are blue" poem you wrote on a card for your mom when you were little or some angsty free verse from your teenage years. It could be good or bad poetry, no judgment.

But have you ever written poetry in form? Iambic pentameter, like Shakespeare? A haiku? A limerick? Most of us stick to free verse because it seems easier. Form feels too rigid and limiting.

Here's the twist: Writing in form can be easier. Constraints provide structure. Like bumper rails for your words, they give your brain something to push against. While at first glance, poetry in form may seem restrictive, it's actually supportive.

You can use this same idea to ignite your imagination. Make up songs that rhyme or write a paragraph about your challenge or opportunity where every sentence has to start with the letter r. I love the concept of the Hemingway six-word story, where you create an entire story in just six words, like his famous story, "For sale: baby shoes, never worn." If you had to put your idea or your best outcome into a six-word story, what would it be?

A friend is an admiral in the US Navy. When her team struggles with improving a process or overcoming an obstacle, her advice to them is always "Make it harder." She finds that the current constraints limit their creativity. Adding even more constraints to make something even harder to solve requires them to completely redefine their approach, which often makes the problem easier to solve.

Bizarro Brainstorming

Sometimes when it's hard to think of anything going right, what if you thought about something going really wrong? This isn't about imagining doom and gloom but rather picturing doing something so poorly that it becomes a farce. Consider employee retention. If you wanted 100 percent employee turnover in a year, what would you have to do to drive employees away? Maybe the employee cafe only served gruel from now on. You could blare sirens at work all day, every day. What if you paid your employees using pennies (or better yet, unrolled pennies)? There are elements of this you can build on to create your ideal solution and let your mind wander there, from office atmosphere to employee compensation. You can apply this technique in many ways at work. If you had to create a new inventory process, what would you do to ensure it was wrong every single time? If you had a certain revenue goal next year, what would the company do to guarantee that you would miss it?

It's just as useful for personal situations. If you wanted to have the worst-ever family road trip, what would you do? You'd bring nothing but black coffee for both the kids and adults to drink. You'd listen to talk radio—loud—from the moment you got in the car until the moment you got out. Everyone in the car would be forced to stay awake at all times and do multiplication tables aloud. It's ridiculous. But it will help you imagine what a great road trip might look like and how you'd prepare.

Shoe Swap

Another great way to engage in imagination is what I call the shoe swap—you step into the shoes of someone else and try to think like they would. I like to "borrow" the brains (and shoes) of people I admire and respect and who may be brilliant in a specific area I need help with. What if you spent fifteen minutes thinking about your next marketing campaign and slid into Taylor Swift's custom, bedazzled Christian Louboutin boots to get her perspective?

You could be struggling with an employee or a leadership challenge, and you call in your best Brené Brown and her "happy shoes."

Perhaps you're having a communication challenge with a family member. What would it be like to put on Mister Rogers's navy Top-Siders?

Or maybe you need some help setting boundaries and handling conflict with grace. Slip into Dolly Parton's rhinestone-studded heels and channel her wisdom: "How can I be kind but not a pushover?"

Imagination isn't a childish indulgence; it's one of our most powerful creative muscles. When we intentionally engage it during moments of stillness, we train our brains to envision new paths forward, be open to possibility, and rehearse our next moves.

EXERCISES

For You: The Possibility Practice

1. **Best-Case Scenario Mapping:** Choose one current challenge or goal. Spend ten minutes imagining the absolute best possible outcome—not just success but wildly exceeding expectations. What would that look like? Feel like? What ripple effects would it create? Let yourself dream without logical constraints.

2. **The Shoe-Swap Solution:** Pick someone you admire (real, fictional, or historical) who embodies qualities you need for a current situation. Spend fifteen minutes literally imagining stepping into their shoes and approaching your challenge from their perspective. What would they notice? How would they respond? What bold moves would they make?

For Your Team: Imagination Unlocked

1. **Reverse-Engineering Failure:** Pick one team goal or challenge. Spend fifteen minutes brainstorming the most ridiculous ways you could guarantee failure (the more absurd, the better). Then flip each "failure strategy" into its positive opposite. Often the most creative solutions emerge from this backward approach.

2. **What-If Wednesday:** Institute a monthly thirty-minute team session where you explore "What if everything went perfectly?" scenarios for upcoming projects or challenges. Create a judgment-free zone where wild possibilities are celebrated, not dismissed. Track which "impossible" ideas contain seeds of workable solutions.

PART 5

SELF-FORGETFULNESS

28

THE JOY OF SELF-FORGETFULNESS

A few years ago, my friend Steve decided to join his church choir. He originally got involved because he thought it might be fun and a good way to meet people. He was right about that, but in the past few years, choir has become so much more to him.

"When I'm singing in a choir, I forget myself. All I can think of is the music, the harmony between the different voice types. Every other thought disappears from my brain, and I get lost in the song," he told me.

Steve's experience in choir is a perfect example of self-forgetfulness, the last step in the continuum to setting the stage for inspiration.

First, we need to create the physical spaciousness we need to clear our minds. Once our minds have the clutter swept up and dumped out, we can focus and be still. In a deep level of stillness, we're able to experience self-forgetfulness. Inspiration doesn't usually strike when we're trying to look impressive or control the outcome. It strikes when we forget to care how we appear at all.

Self-forgetfulness is exactly what it suggests—we forget ourselves. Our focus and attention are elsewhere and we're not worried about how we look or sound, we're not conscious of how we appear in a room, we're fully present and almost outside of our bodies.

I always think of self-forgetfulness like a spotlight. Most people train the spotlight on themselves as they go about their day. We hear our own thought and think about what we have to do next or where we need to be. We are the protagonists, the main characters, of our own story. When we're experiencing self-forgetfulness, that spotlight swings around. We are no longer the star of our own lives—someone or something else has taken center stage.

Self-forgetfulness doesn't mean an absolute loss of self or ego. In this way, the term can be misleading. It's a state in which we are so focused and still that we lose our sense of self.

At first glance, self-forgetfulness may seem like spaciousness or stillness. You'd think that if you were totally absorbed in an activity that you may completely forget yourself, but this is not always the case. Absorption, the state of being we reach through stillness, can include a heightened sense of self. You might become absorbed rehearsing a speech or writing a bio for an article or a website; in both cases, you monitor yourself. Self-forgetfulness removes the mirror. You're fully present, but you're not watching yourself.

Self-forgetfulness is a beautiful place to be. Mental chatter silences. The twelve-lane highway of fast-moving thoughts in our brains slows down to a meandering country road. When we stop focusing on ourselves, we gain a greater sense of connection, engagement, and immersion in the present moment.

Forgetting about yourself, temporarily, is a gift. You lose the weight of self-consciousness to slip fully into the present. It's not ego death—it's ego quiet. The part of you that's always narrating, strategizing, or self-critiquing goes silent for a little while. In that quiet, you find clarity, connection, and sometimes, the earliest flickers of inspiration.

Considered a different way, self-forgetfulness leads to connection. When we swing the spotlight around, the light illuminates life outside ourselves. In that state, we can feel a deep sense of connection with community, with nature, with art, or with something larger. Over the next few chapters, we'll explore how to slip into self-forgetfulness, whether through community, nature, art, journaling, or travel.

Recognizing Your Self-Forgetfulness Moments

Self-forgetfulness isn't something you can force—you're not observing yourself, you only notice it afterward. Think back over your recent experiences and identify when you might have slipped into this state.

Physical Signs

» Time seemed to disappear or move differently.

» You weren't aware of your body's position or comfort.

» You forgot to check your phone or think about other tasks.

Mental Signs

» Your internal narrator went quiet.

» You weren't worried about how you looked or sounded.

» Problems or anxieties temporarily vanished from your mind.

Emotional Signs

» You felt deeply connected to something beyond yourself.

» There was no sense of performing or being watched.

» You felt a lightness or expansion in your chest.

Common Self-Forgetfulness Triggers: What activities, settings, or circumstances have created these moments for you? Was it during conversation, creative work, physical activity, time in nature, or moments of service to others?

The goal isn't to manufacture self-forgetfulness but to recognize when it happens naturally and notice what conditions make it more likely. In the upcoming chapters, we'll explore specific pathways that open these doorways to inspiration.

29

THE COLLECTIVE SPARK

In *Man's Search for Meaning*, Victor Frankl writes, "The more one forgets himself—by giving himself to a cause to serve or another person to love—the more human he is and the more he actualizes himself."

And honestly, I think that's it. That's the ballgame.

The third precursor to inspiration, self-forgetfulness, captures exactly that. It involves getting so caught up in something so meaningful, so much bigger than yourself, that you stop performing.

Inspiration goes beyond great ideas. At its best, it starts to transform us into who we're meant to be. Not the hustling, image-conscious version of ourselves, but the real version—the one who wears a retainer at night, sings off-key carpool karaoke with the windows down, and snort-laughs. When we feel inspired, something bigger takes the stage. We step outside ourselves and forget ourselves completely.

One of the easiest places to find self-forgetfulness is in community.

There's a kind of magic that happens when we're in the right room with the right people for the right reasons. The weight of worry that we carry about how we're perceived, how we perform, or whether we're "doing it right" gets a little lighter. Something bigger moves into the foreground, and for a moment, we forget ourselves.

In the case of community, that "something bigger" might be a shared goal, a group experience, a message that hits home, or a moment of deep resonance and connection with others.

When we're in the right room, whether it's a worship service, a Brazilian jujitsu class, a leadership group, or a Springsteen concert, we're not sitting in our own heads, narrating our shortcomings or worrying what someone thinks of us. We're absorbed in the moment, especially in the collective. We think less about "me" and more about "we."

We often think of inspiration as a solo act, experienced while walking alone in the woods or sitting by ourselves. Inspiration can happen when you're alone, yes, but just as often, it arrives in the hum of togetherness, in the spaces where we're seen, challenged, encouraged, and reminded that we're part of something larger than ourselves.

Volunteering and nonprofit work can be inspiring. Ross, a client of mine, donated some of his deceased father's furniture to a local nonprofit, Humble Design, that furnishes homes for people transitioning out of homelessness. He was invited to participate in a Day of Joy, in which volunteers work with staff to move in furniture and decorate a home for a client. The nonprofit team was going to use Ross's family's furniture for the new home. Ross told the story of how seeing those familiar pieces of furniture used for a new purpose moved him deeply. He thought more about the cause, the new purpose for this furniture than about his family or himself. This profound experience of self-forgetfulness tied Ross and his family to helping the homelessness and to the organization, Humble Design, itself.

Think about a retreat where everyone is there to grow, learn, or rest. Think about a concert where everyone belts out the same lyrics. Think about a peer advisory board where the leader sitting across from you is sharing a story so raw and honest that you stop rehearsing your own response and just listen. Inspiration also blooms in these spaces.

When we're in the right type of community, we engage with people who have similar values, interests, or goals, and there's an unspoken agreement: We're in this together. This alignment of purpose provides fertile soil for inspiration. We find these types of environments everywhere in religious communities and community councils, knitting circles and pickleball leagues, book clubs and rock bands, artist guilds and improv groups. These groups can meet in person or virtually. Participating in these groups, in the discussions or meetings, often leads us to think outside ourselves.

Priya Parker wrote a gorgeous book, *The Art of Gathering*, and in it, she talks about committing to gathering about *something*—the best gatherings have a purpose. And with that purpose comes a sense of belonging. And in that belonging, we can step outside of ourselves and come closer to the spark of inspiration.

It's not just about the big, obvious inspiration. The spark can come quietly through watching someone else navigate a challenge with grace, hearing a story that cracks your heart open, or witnessing someone else's courage that reminds you of your own.

Let's bring the idea of community to the corporate setting. I work with a few pest control companies. Roaches, rats, and bed bugs are not most people's idea of a good time, nor the first place that many people think to apply for a job. One of these companies has an employee retention rate that's twice the national average. Why? Because they hire and lead with three simple values: family, care, and security. Employees feel like they're part of something. Customers are treated like family. And the work, while not glamorous, is meaningful. The community they've built inspires people to stay, to care, to go the extra mile.

Contrast that to an organization full of silos and politics. Amazon has been widely criticized for having a culture that promotes internal competition over collaboration. Employees are graded on a curve, and low performers are regularly cut. The system breeds siloed teams, promotes internal politics, and leads to what some describe as a "hire to fire" philosophy. Amazon tops the ranks of US companies with the worst employee retention rates.

Organizations where everyone is covering their butt and watching their back are not places where we'll find inspiration. In those environments, people are too busy self-protecting to self-forget.

Self-forgetfulness requires safety, value alignment, and a willingness to participate rather than simply observe. When we're watching from the sidelines, maybe because the environment doesn't feel safe or aligned, we stay in our heads. When we create safe spaces where people feel welcome, safe, and seen, they engage—and feel like they belong. A feeling of belonging allows them to more easily swing that spotlight to something outside themselves and opens the gate for inspiration more easily.

Community needs just a few key ingredients to create the conditions for self-forgetfulness:

> » a shared sense of purpose and values, with a "why" that feels bigger than any one person
>
> » a culture of safety, vulnerability, and authenticity
>
> » a spirit of welcome and inclusion

When those elements are in place, community becomes fertile ground for inspiration. We lose ourselves in the right way in service to something meaningful and connective.

When we're able to forget ourselves like that, we often find something else in return: clarity, hope, courage, a new idea, or a next step.

EXERCISES:

For You: Community Mapping

1. **Your Connection Audit:** List the communities where you currently feel genuine belonging (e.g., work teams, hobby groups, faith communities, volunteer organizations). Next to each, note what specific elements make you feel safe to be authentic—shared values, vulnerability, acceptance, common purpose?

2. **The Belonging Gap:** Identify one area of your life where you wish you felt more connected to community. What's one concrete step you could take this month to either deepen an existing connection or explore a new community that aligns with your values or interests?

For Your Team: Building Community Through Service

1. **Values-Based Volunteering:** Ask team members to share causes or organizations they care about. Look for overlap and plan a quarterly team volunteer day with an organization that reflects shared values. Focus on the collective impact rather than team building for its own sake.

2. **The Safety Check:** During your next team meeting, ask, "When do you feel most able to be authentic and contribute your best thinking here?" and "What would make our team feel more like the kind of community where people can forget about protecting themselves and focus on the work?" Use responses to identify specific changes that could increase psychological safety.

30

WHEN NATURE
MAKES YOU FORGET YOURSELF

Have you ever stood at the edge of the Grand Canyon and felt your problems shrink to the size of pebbles? Or watched a thunderstorm roll in and suddenly realized you were holding your breath, completely forgetting the argument you'd been replaying in your head? Hiked a trail where the trees felt older than your worries? Looked at a ridgeline so vast that your deadlines dissolved?

When the world becomes big and you become small, you experience self-forgetfulness. Nature is one of the most reliable places to lose yourself in something bigger.

We've already talked about nature's power to create spaciousness and stillness, how it clears mental clutter and quiets racing thoughts. But nature also does something else when it comes to self-forgetfulness. It doesn't just calm your mind or give you breathing room; it puts you in your place in the best possible way.

The natural world creates that feeling of self-forgetfulness because it's so much bigger than we are. In its vastness, we forget who we are. Feeling that we are in the presence of something greater than ourselves quickly shifts our perspective from an internal focus to an external focus.

When we're caught up in our daily lives, we're the protagonists of our own stories. Every slight feels personal, every deadline feels critical, every decision feels monumental. We live in a world scaled to human concerns.

Then we step outside the human-sized world and encounter something vast. The Pacific Ocean stretching beyond the horizon, a night sky dense with stars, a forest where the trees have been growing since before your great-grandparents were born. Suddenly that presentation you've been losing sleep over doesn't loom so large. The conflict with your colleague seems less earth-shattering. The spotlight normally trained on your thoughts and worries swings outward illuminating something immeasurably larger.

This isn't about us invalidating ourselves, our challenges, hardships, or worries. It's about a shift in perspective. When you feel genuinely small in the presence of something vast, you remember that you're part of a much bigger story. That remembering is self-forgetfulness.

When we examine what happens to help us make that shift, there are two feelings tied most closely to our experiences in nature: awe and wonder.

Awe is what happens when you encounter something so magnificent that it stops you in your tracks. It's that gasp when you crest a hill and see an endless vista. It's the way your thoughts go quiet when you watch waves crash against an ancient cliff.

A 2015 Stanford study found that walking in nature reduced rumination, the repetitive, negative thoughts that cycle in our brains. The researchers measured both self-reporting and brain activity in the subgenual prefrontal cortex. That's the area of our brains just behind our eyes that helps us regulate our mood, especially processing emotion, regulating negative thoughts, controlling stress responses, and connecting emotional and physical response. Nature helps people get out of their own heads.

But awe does more than just clear away our mental clutter. Two other studies, one in the *Journal of Personality and Social Psychology* and one in a 2023 review by Keltner and Monroy, show that awe not only makes us more generous and induces ethical behavior, it also strengthens social connection, reduces inflammation, and boosts oxytocin, also known as "the bonding hormone" because it's released during connection and helps to calm the nervous system. When we feel awe, we're less focused on ourselves and more focused on others. Walking in nature not only calms us, it also makes us better humans.

Awe grounds you in the present moment. It fills you with gratitude instead of anxiety, with peace rather than restlessness. In those moments, instead of seeing yourself as the center of the universe, you see yourself as a part of a larger system, a small, connected piece of something magnificent.

If awe is the thunderclap that rattles us into reverence, wonder is the soft hum that makes us tilt our heads and smile. Awe says, "Woah!" and wonder says, "Huh, how interesting." Nature can give us both.

Wonder is what you feel watching a hummingbird hover in midair, its wings beating so fast they're invisible. It's the curiosity that bubbles up when you notice that the morning light filters differently through a maple than an oak leaf. It's the gentle amazement at discovering the weed in your sidewalk is growing tiny, perfect flowers.

A state of wonder has a sense of joy and lightness to it unlike the grounding feeling we get with awe. Where awe can feel almost overwhelming in intensity, wonder feels joyful and playful. It's closer to a childlike sense of curiosity, endlessly fascinated by how things work, why they happen, and what might be possible.

Both awe and wonder accomplish the same thing—pulling your attention from your internal narrative and directing it outside yourself.

Awe and wonder feel less uniquely personal and individual-ized than a shared vision or goal. It's true that an ornithologist may feel more wonder at the flight of a hummingbird than a regular person, or an oceanographer may feel tremendous awe at the power of the sea. Our own personal filters affect what makes us feel both awe and wonder, but both of those emotional states are loosely tied to our personal values, our dreams, and our goals. This depersonalization makes it easier to feel a sense of self-forgetfulness. Wonder and awe clear the boundaries of our brains so that we are more open and make more space for inspi-ration to potentially appear.

You don't need to trek to Everest base camp to experience awe or wonder. You access both by simply noticing nature, whether you're looking at the intricacy of a spider web or watching a bird build a nest in the rafters above the parking structure. You might find it stepping outside for a break between meetings to listen to the wind in the trees or the buzz of summer bugs.

Every 120 seconds of intentional attention to the natural world reduces cortisol, increases your focus, and makes that abil-ity to tap into awe and wonder that much easier. That's shorter than some terrible TikTok recipe videos.

One CEO I work with, Tanya, has started taking walking meetings outside.

"I swear I have better ideas, deeper conversations, and a sharper ability to solve problems when there are trees in view and no ceilings in sight," she told me. "Something about being under the sky instead of under fluorescent lights changes how I think about problems. They shrink in size."

When you're truly present with nature, the mental clutter clears. The constant self-monitoring quiets down. You stop wor-rying about how you look, what you should be doing, or what others might think.

You forget yourself in the best possible way.

In forgetting, you often find clarity about what truly matters, perspectives on challenges that seemed insurmountable, or simply a connection with something larger than yourself.

Of course you can't escape your concerns permanently, but you can step outside of them long enough to gain perspective, to remember that you're part of something larger, and to create space for fresh insights to emerge. Whether you're standing under a cathedral of redwoods or watching a bee dip in and out of a flower, the mental clutter clears, the judgment softens, and you slip outside of yourself. And that's often the place you find exactly what you were looking for.

EXERCISES

For You: The Small Practice

1. **Seek Your Awe Spot:** Find one place within fifteen minutes of your home or office where you can feel genuinely small—under a big sky, next to an old tree, near moving water, or overlooking a wide view. Visit it this week when you're stuck in self-focused thinking. Notice how this creates small shifts in your perspective on current challenges.

2. **Wonder Hunting:** For five days, spend three minutes each day actively seeking something in nature that sparks curiosity. How does that spider web stay so perfectly geometric? Why do those clouds form that particular shape? What makes that bird choose that specific branch? After the exercise, think about moments when you stopped thinking about yourself and started wondering about what you're observing.

For Your Team: Perspective Shifting

1. **The Humbling Meeting:** Hold one team meeting outside with the most expansive natural view accessible from your workplace, even if it's just a parking lot with open sky. Spend three minutes in silence looking up or out before discussing business. Notice how the shift in scale affects the conversation about workplace challenges.

2. **Shared Wonder Check-ins:** Start one meeting per month by having everyone share something from nature that recently caught their attention and made them curious (not just "It was pretty" but "I wondered how/why . . ."). Notice how the conversation shifts when people talk about wonder rather than work problems.

31

ART

Most of us don't have a museum in the break room, and most corporate art is somewhere between "bland meadow" and "beige blur." Even so, art has a way of sneaking up on us. Have you ever walked through a gallery or a museum and been absolutely taken by a painting or a photograph? Perhaps a majestic willow tree photographed in black and white that made you just stop and ponder it. Maybe it was the smooth lines of a bronze sculpture. Outside of a museum, you might be struck by the opening passage of a book or introduction of a favorite song. You could be wowed by the beauty of a costume in a play or the cinematography in a movie. Art can show up in the way a dish is plated at your favorite restaurant. We can forget ourselves just as easily in art as we can in nature.

To briefly backtrack, we know spaciousness is a state of being that leads to inspiration. Spaciousness is a sense of openness in both our environments and our minds. In psychological terms, this state maps closely to a personality trait called openness to experience, part of the Big Five personality framework. This trait makes us curious, imaginative, and willing to explore new ideas. Within the broader category lives a more specific gem, openness to aesthetics. That's our capacity to connect deeply with art, beauty, and sensory experiences. It's also one of the easiest on-ramps to self-forgetfulness.

While openness to aesthetics is a personality trait (meaning you may be more or less open on a continuous scale as part of your personality makeup), the experience is available to anyone. People who score higher on the scale are more likely to lose themselves in the presence of art, but that doesn't mean if you score lower on the scale that you can't lose yourself in art too.

You can experience openness to aesthetics in galleries or museums, while you read, or when you make your own art. Science backs that up.

A study from Cambridge University in 2025 had museum visitors engage with minimalist art and instructed them to focus on either the beauty of the art or performing a task matching each ceramic object they saw to a line drawing. Those focused on beauty were 14 percent more likely to think abstractly and also reported feeling "moved" or "inspired."

Reading can bring about stillness, and depending on the writing, it can also help us tap into our openness to aesthetics, and by doing so, our self-forgetfulness. Some writers bring about a sense of awe through their word choice or imagery, or via the rhythm of their sentences.

You can also feel this sense of selflessness when you engage in making your own art. As you create with a brush or a saw, a thread or with your own hands, and you see something take shape, begin to come to life, you can drop into that feeling of stillness and self-forgetfulness.

Combining both community and art can create an even deeper feeling of self-forgetfulness—like my friend Steve experienced while singing in the choir. There is also something to be said about communities that rally around art of any kind. We can connect to a deep sense of selflessness when we are engrossed in what psychologists refer to as an "aesthetic experience." I have a friend who feels a deep sense of community when she hears an orchestra tuning up prior to a performance.

I'll personally vouch for that; I, too, feel a great sense of community at concerts and shows. I'm moved by a group of people who come together to experience something that they love, find great joy in, feel understood or seen or heard, have memories of or with, with chords that make them sway, stomp, and sing.

Let me tell you about the Boss.

I spent the first years of my life in New Jersey, and like most good guardians of the Garden State, my blood is about 30 percent Bruce. Attending a Springsteen concert is like stepping into a stadium-sized heartbeat. Thousands of strangers join together, belting out the same lyrics, fists pumping in time with the music, maybe hollering for just the right chord change. It's church. It's therapy. It's electric.

In those moments I'm not a coach, a keynote speaker, or someone who left dishes in the sink. I'm not wondering if my gray roots are showing. I am just . . . gone. Lost in the music, the crowd, the sheer humanness of it all. That's the magic.

How do we bring that magic out of the stadium or studio and into the office?

You can put art up on your office or cubicle walls or in a small frame on your desk. You can tap into digital art on a host of different websites or during your lunch break, taking advantage of the virtual tours that some museums offer, whether the Metropolitan Museum of Art or the Vatican.

Again, we can look beyond visual art. Some people find the aesthetic in writing—working on a speech or an article or a LinkedIn post that feels good to you. You could find it in a perfectly styled presentation or a piece of collateral where you get to really sink into visual design. For others, numbers are art, and you relish your time engrossed in a well-made spreadsheet or in neat lines of code.

The keys here are noticing and appreciating. Simply noticing, which we also experience in stillness, helps us get out of our own brains. We can go to a deeper level of self-forgetfulness when we take time to notice details, especially in art. The same goes for appreciating. Appreciating is a deeper version of noticing—taking the time to stop and really sink into something so that we can see it in its best light. In *The Art of Noticing*, Rob Walker talks about noticing and reframing the beauty of a traffic cone. We may take it for granted or not see any beauty in it, but when we really look at it, we can take ourselves out of our own brains by reframing what we see and notice, and turn it into appreciation.

Engaging deeply with authentic, meaningful artwork in the form that speaks most to us shifts our attention from "me" to "we," sparking self-forgetfulness, empathy, and inspiration. We know it also expands cognitive framing by allowing us to think more abstractly and shift our perspective on things. Most important, it primes the pump for inspiration by momentarily quieting the reflexive self.

EXERCISES

For You: Your Aesthetic Pathway

1. **Beauty Archaeology:** Think back to the last time a piece of art (e.g., visual, musical, written, or performance) made you completely lose track of time or forget your surroundings. What was it about that experience that pulled you out of yourself? How can you seek more of that type of aesthetic experience?

2. **The Reframing Challenge:** Choose something mundane in your daily environment (like Rob Walker's traffic cone) and spend five minutes finding three elements of beauty or design in it. Notice how shifting from dismissal to appreciation changes your mental state and pulls focus away from internal chatter.

For Your Team: Collective Aesthetic Moments

1. **Art That Moves Us:** During your next team meeting, ask everyone to share one piece of art (broadly defined—music, film, visual art, design, even a beautifully crafted presentation) that made them forget about everything else for a few minutes. What patterns emerge in what moves your team members?

2. **Office Beauty Hunt:** Challenge the team to identify one overlooked element of beauty or good design in your workplace (e.g., architecture, lighting, even the way someone organized their desk). Share discoveries in your next meeting. How does actively seeking beauty shift the team's relationship to their environment?

32

FLEXIBLE DISCIPLINE

Have you ever promised yourself you'd get back into shape? Most of us have probably made that commitment to ourselves at some point. We're going to lose the belly fat, tone our arms, or improve our cardio so we're not short of breath going up a long flight of stairs.

We commit to start going to the gym five days a week, for an hour each time, but since we haven't gone to the gym in months, this schedule seems overwhelming.

When Monday rolls around and it's time to head to the gym after work, wouldn't you know it, our meetings that day run long. Tuesday, an old friend invites us out for drinks. We say yes because we want to reconnect. We successfully make it to the gym on Wednesday, skip Thursday because we feel sick, then squeeze in a quick treadmill session on Friday.

Instead of celebrating the two days that we went to the gym, we beat ourselves up about the three days we didn't. We tell ourselves we don't have enough time to go to the gym, or we spiral into shame about our lack of consistency. That initial motivation transforms into self-criticism, making us wonder, What's the point? Soon we're back to zero gym days.

What if we shifted our commitment? Instead of a rigid gym schedule, we commit to moving our bodies five days a week.

Some days that's an hour at the gym, and other days we take a long walk with the dog, stretching or doing a few sets of air squats and sit-ups when time is tight.

We make progress, not in grand gestures or unachievable goals but in the commitment to showing up every day in whatever way is available to us.

In *Atomic Habits*, James Clear does a beautiful job of explaining the psychology behind habits. The key to creating a habit is consistency. In the getting-back-into-shape example, successful habit formation relies less on showing up at the squat rack every day at 6:30 p.m. and more on a commitment to moving our bodies that day in whatever way works for us.

I like to refer to this as "flexible discipline." We can use that same flexible discipline to create spaciousness and stillness, and foster a sense of self-forgetfulness. It's less important how we engage in those practices and more important that we simply engage on a regular basis.

Writers talk a lot about "the Muse," the mythical being that shows up for creatives and helps them create. Writers understand that the Muse rewards consistency and that the more often you show up, the more often she shows up. She doesn't come to every writing session. Sometimes you're left to army crawl through a few pages to just get your words and ideas down on the page. You feel a little battered and bruised after those writing sessions. But when the Muse does show up, the writing sessions feel effortless, almost like you're not the one writing at all. Words and ideas course through your fingers, and your only job is to keep up and get it all down on paper.

The Muse doesn't care if you show up for five minutes a day or five hours a day; what she does care about is that you show up EVERY day. She wants to see that you have a practice, that you're committed to your work. In mythology, the Muse rewards those who show their resolve and discipline with the consistency of their actions. She'd rather see your ass in the chair working on a writing project for thirty minutes at lunch every day than putting in four hours every other weekend.

The Muse in inspiration is no different. She cares less about your taking one weekend a year practicing the pillars of inspiration, and more about your taking ten minutes per day. You may get a ton of ideas during that one weekend when you've allowed yourself to shut out the world, but how great would it be to apply that power regularly?

When we are training our bodies or brains to do anything, or when we're forming a habit, it's the muscle memory, the repetition, that builds our skillsets. Spaciousness, stillness, and self-forgetfulness aren't things we earn and are allowed to keep forever. Just like getting in shape, they're practices we work at and return to again and again. When we protect the time for spaciousness, stillness, and self-forgetfulness, the Muse of Inspiration slips in and whispers her wisdom and brilliance into our ears.

How can you create that flexible discipline for yourself?

Maybe the time you carve out for your pre-inspiration practice varies by the day. Some days you can find it first thing in the morning, and other days you carve a block of time during lunch or later in the evening, after the busyness of the day has settled down. You may find that while on paper, it looks easier to set aside time to yourself midmorning, but it turns out that it's easier after lunch. Or you may find your brain is too full any time after noon, and it's easier to clear it during another time of day. Some people love the stillness of early morning and of dusk. Those two periods are when their minds are the most settled: as the sun first peeks over the horizon and when it slowly sinks in delicate periwinkle skies at the end of the day. Be curious about what works best for you and know that it may change over time.

The amount of time that you spend in practice can also vary by day. If you control your calendar, you may be able to block a solid hour of undisturbed time every day. But most people don't have that level of control over their day. So some days you've got ten minutes dedicated to slowing the superhighway of thoughts in your brain, and other days you have an hour or more. I'd recommend setting a minimum amount of time for practice every day. Maybe your minimum is five or ten minutes. (It's hard to experience true spaciousness, stillness, and self-forgetfulness in less time than that. We normally spend the first few moments chasing the thoughts from our brains.) The quality of time spent in creating this practice is more important than the quantity of time.

To be clear, creating time and space for this practice isn't just one more thing to check off your list. If you're not careful, we can turn even a sacred practice into a productivity hack. The goal here is not to optimize but to listen and make space for what's trying to emerge.

The methods you use to build your practice can also vary. Some days your pre-inspiration practice may center around engaging in a hobby, working on a woodworking project, or gardening. Other days you find it while you're out on a walk.

Flexible discipline requires daily effort. You might allow yourself a day or two off per week, but otherwise you're showing up, in whatever way works best for you on that specific day. We make progress in the consistency and the discipline of setting the time aside regularly. We also need to be careful that the one day off doesn't turn into two or three. But if we allow ourselves flexibility in the way we set aside time to show up for ourselves every day, we're more likely to encounter inspiration.

What I love most about flexible discipline is that it requires grace. You'll miss a day. You'll get distracted. That's not failure; it's the friction of transformation. You just have to keep coming back.

Setting the stage for inspiration doesn't demand perfection. It doesn't require a mountaintop, a sound bath, or a silent retreat. The Muse of Inspiration doesn't need hours and hours, just consistent attention. When we show up daily with flexible discipline, we build a pattern that allows insight to thread itself into our lives.

EXERCISES

For You: Flexible Discipline Blueprint

1. Set a daily minimum for stillness time.

2. Pick a time of day that feels most attainable.

3. Outline three different ways you're going to start to achieve stillness.

4. Mark a calendar or use an accountability system that works for you.

5. Write your "why"—what makes this practice worth pursuing and protecting?

For Your Team: Daily Disconnect Practice

1. Set out the same questions and parameters as in the Flexible Discipline Blueprint exercise above.

2. At the end of the week, ask each team member to share an insight, a benefit, or a failure.

PART 6

FIVE ELEMENTS OF AN INSPIRATIONAL STORY

33

THE INSPIRATION CHART

The most transformative moments in human experience don't happen in isolation; they emerge from the stories we tell one another. Think about the last time you felt truly moved to change something in your life. Chances are it wasn't from reading statistics or advice but from listening to, learning from, or watching someone walk through something hard, something messy, and something real and emerge transformed. In a recent survey I conducted, over 90 percent of respondents reported being inspired by stories. Inspirational stories have an almost magnetic power to shift something within us.

Story is our oldest technology for change. Oral language predates written language by eons. Long before we had data visualization or motivation frameworks, we had the simple, profound act of one person telling another: "Here's what happened to me. Here's what I learned. Here's how I'm different now."

Science supports this. Research by the psychologists at York University in Toronto found that narrative stories are more easily understood and better recalled than expository, essay-like texts. But memory is just the beginning. Stories don't just lodge in our minds; they reshape how we see ourselves and what we believe is possible. Inspirational stories often reframe challenges to opportunities, help listeners commit to their own visions, and translate abstract concepts into tangible experiences, sparking listeners to pursue their goals and embrace change. These stories can come from a 12-step meeting or a TED talk. No matter their source, they transform the abstract into the visceral and the theoretical into the urgent.

After years of listening to, reading, watching, and witnessing inspirational stories, both in my coaching practice and in personal life, I've noticed a pattern. The stories that really move us, that inspire us to take action, all have the same emotional blueprint. While no two stories are the same, they all include five key ingredients.

The first ingredient is courage. In inspirational stories, we see someone exhibit courage in the face of fear, whether that's overcoming an outside adversary or an internal fear.

The second ingredient is hardship. There's a challenge or an obstacle to be overcome. The main character of the story experiences adversity of some kind.

The third ingredient is authenticity. Not only do the facts of the story need to be true, but the person telling the story needs to believe them.

The fourth ingredient is resilience. Inspirational stories, especially those that inspire us to action, include someone who rises to the challenge again and again.

The fifth and final ingredient is transformation. In an inspirational narrative, the protagonist is changed in some way.

I call it the CHART framework:

- » Courage
- » Hardship
- » Authenticity
- » Resilience
- » Transformation

When we CHART our course from what's possible to what's probable, we trace a path of growth and meaning. Someone steps into courage while facing hardship, they share honestly, choose resilience, and as a result, they transform.

In the chapters ahead, we'll examine each of these elements, looking at how you can use them to tell your own story, whether you're speaking on stage, leading a team, raising a child, or just trying to inspire yourself to keep going. These five elements will help you craft a narrative to inspire.

In addition to the descriptions, each chapter will also include exercises for you to try. These exercises look a little different than the ones you've seen earlier. In previous sections, we split them into "For You" and "For Your Team." But because the five elements of an inspirational story apply equally to your personal life and your business, we've designed this set to bridge both. You'll find exercises for *you as a person* and *you as a leader of a business.*

34

COURAGE

The firefighters of Engine 54/Ladder 4/Battalion 9 in New York City driving to the twin towers on 9/11. Ruby Bridges attending her first day of school at an all-white elementary school in New Orleans while throngs of protestors yell and grab at her clothing in 1960. Mahatma Gandhi's leading 240 people on the Salt March to Dandi in India to protest British imperialism in 1930. Irena Sendler saving thousands of children from the Nazis in Poland in the early '40s. The Lost Boys of Sudan walking a thousand miles across harsh terrain to reach safety in the late '80s. Dr. Christine Blasey Ford testifying in front of Congress about her sexual assault, knowing what it would cost her in 2018. These are big moments of courage that took place on a national or international stage.

We also see quiet examples of courage every day: a person leaving an abusive relationship, an addict admitting they need help, a cancer patient shaving their head before the start of chemotherapy. Why is courage so important in an inspirational story? Because fear holds us back. Inevitably there are things in our life that we'd love to accomplish, but they seem bigger than us. These goals and dreams seem out of reach and unattainable. We may not be sure we have the skills or ability to achieve our goal, we may feel like it's too late in life to accomplish it, or we may worry about being judged by friends, families, colleagues, or community. We might worry about rejection or failure.

The common thread is fear. We're terrified. Scared. On the surface we may look calm. Rather than a rolling boil of fear, we experience a quiet simmer. In fact, it's so quiet that we may not even notice that the fear is there. And fear may wear a disguise. Fear can show up like procrastination, perfectionism, indecision, or avoidance. It can also present as insecurity or anger. So we dismiss it. Regardless of how it shows up, fear can hobble even the strongest among us.

That's where courage comes in. Courage is the ability to confront all of those emotions—fear, uncertainty, doubt, danger—and to act anyway. To go back to school after the kids have left the house. To go for the big job. To travel internationally by ourselves. To learn to sail when we're afraid of water.

Many of the stories that inspire us involve people confronting powerful forces with life, liberty, and freedom at stake, whether that's the Mahatma Gandhis or the Ruby Bridges of the world. But in many other stories we find inspirational, the strongest enemy the protagonist faced was the judge and critic living within.

Our greatest moments of courage may happen when we stand up to the fear inside ourselves.

Courage shows up everywhere and in all different facets of life. It's a kid in middle school raising their hand in class to say they don't understand something. It's a leader saying, "I was wrong," in public. Emotional courage is asking for what you need in a relationship instead of pretending you're fine. Social courage is saying "I'm sorry" or "I forgive you" and really meaning it. Professional courage is turning down a client who doesn't align with your culture or ideals, even if you need the revenue. Courage could be letting yourself be seen without armor or polish. You can have courage setting boundaries and learning to say "No" as a complete sentence. You may show courage in a big life transition or becoming a caregiver for someone you love (or for someone you don't).

The words *brave* and *courageous* are often used interchangeably, but they're different. Bravery assumes fearlessness— the absence of fear. The same kind of fearlessness that we see in superhero movies, where our heroes go off to fight the enemy and save the world. We know what's at stake, and while we may see those heroes express sadness, regret, or potentially anger, we rarely see the fear.

Don't get me wrong; we're still rooting for them. We still cheer when they beat the bad guys. But how often do they inspire us? How often do we look at those heroes, even some of whom are human, and see ourselves in them? Especially when that character lacks any feeling of fear?

My colleague Rachel sat in a large networking meeting a few years ago. Most of the people around the table knew each other well. Each month, the group leader asked a different inclusion question, and the question for that meeting was, "What's your greatest fear?"

Most people in the room were up to the challenge, and they went deep with their responses. There were answers like "dying alone" or "my kids getting sick or dying." Other people spoke of a fear of being homeless, or of heights, of water. Most of the room, maybe twenty-five people or so, had provided their answers, and it came to one last participant. Let's call him Jim. And when called upon to share his greatest fear, he answered, "I'm not afraid of anything. Maybe that's why I'm so good at my job," and proceeded to recite his traditional spiel about his role and his business.

To be fair, maybe Jim truly does not have any fears. I'm sure it's possible. But the mood shifted dramatically. Rachel said it was almost like those twenty-second-floor conference room windows blew out and all the trust rushed out like a gasp. Jim, who was earnestly telling of a client's success under his tutelage, with no situational awareness, had lost the room. His story of how he had helped a client in dire need, the hero's story, wasn't the least bit inspiring. How do you trust someone who's not willing to be vulnerable? How do you inspire others when you don't admit to fear?

We aren't inspired by the absence of fear; we're inspired by those who dance with it. The most moving stories don't make us think, "Wow, I could never do that." They make us think, "Maybe I could." Courage closes the gap between impossibility and action.

Putting the Framework to Use:

>> **Personal:** Think of a time you acted despite fear. What was the fear, and what action did you take anyway? Write one paragraph on how it changed you.

>> **Business:** Recall a decision your organization made that required courage. What was at stake, and what did you gain from acting anyway?

35

HARDSHIP

No one would have written about Odysseus if he'd stayed home from the war and tended his garden. We wouldn't have seen Neo defy physics in *The Matrix* had he chosen the blue pill. If not for evil Uncle Scar and the death of Mufasa, none of us would know Simba from *The Lion King*.

Inspirational stories aren't built on fame, brilliance, or the perfect plan that's been executed flawlessly. They often entail confidence-shaking, gut-punching, how-will-I-survive-this hardship. The kinds of challenges that keep you under the covers or make you want to cry.

Or quit.

Hardship is often the first element that people name when talking about stories that inspire them. The protagonist has overcome something difficult, physically, mentally, or emotionally, and has lived to tell the tale about it. These heroes may be people we know personally or historical figures or famous people.

Some people face overwhelming adversity, like Victor Frankl surviving Nazi concentration camps during the Holocaust, Malala Yousafzai surviving a murder attempt by the Taliban for advocating for girls' education in Pakistan, or Harriet Tubman conducting nearly seventy people through the underground railroad to escape slavery. These are all hardships with a capital *H*.

Adversity on a smaller scale can be just as inspiring: an adult who never finished college and works full-time during the day and studies at night to get their degree; a recent widower, grieving alone, who finally reaches out to a grief group for support; an employee terrified of public speaking who commits to giving a toast at a team event—and nails it.

All of these stories feature real moments of doubt. We can see that the deck is stacked against that person and that their ability to overcome isn't guaranteed.

Think about a story with no challenge or hurdle. If something is "easy" for someone, and they accomplish it, we are much less likely to be inspired by them.

Joseph Campbell's Hero's Journey is the perfect example of how adversity plays out in inspirational narratives. It's a common storytelling structure that we see in everything from epic poems like *The Odyssey* to movies like *Forrest Gump*. These are stories of ordinary people living their lives, who get pulled into something or face something bigger than they imagined, walk through fire (sometimes literally), and then emerge transformed.

The structure of the Hero's Journey comprises three stages; in the middle stage, the main character goes through trials and tribulations, getting to the crux of their challenges or "the ordeal."

In *The Odyssey*, Odysseus is trying to get home to his wife and son after a decade of fighting in the Trojan War. The gods have other plans for him, and he spends another ten years battling sea monsters, cursed winds, and cyclopes to get home. Forrest Gump is searching for adventure, and it finds him. Whether it's Vietnam, Mama's death, or Jenny leaving, he faces adversity and relies on his mother's advice to get him through.

The adversity makes these stories inspirational.

We've all seen photos of a CEO standing proudly on stage at the New York Stock Exchange grinning as they ring the bell to mark their company's first day as a publicly traded entity. While the moment itself is inspiring, how much more powerful is it if we know there's been hardship along the way, like the time the company lost their biggest customer, had a total of forty-seven dollars in the bank, and got hit with a lawsuit but stuck it out to become the success it is today? Is the story of being listed on the NYSE inspiring all on its own? Potentially. But with the addition of the adversity and the implied persistence (the company is still around and successful, so we know that the founders pushed through), doesn't it become even more inspirational? How does it change if the CEO was born into privilege, and had parents and their friends as investors and backers, who put money into the company any time there was risk or a downturn? It doesn't take away from the success of the day, but it may make it less inspiring to other struggling entrepreneurs.

Hardship is the heckler in the stands, the storm in the middle of the journey, the voice that says, "You're not good enough." Every inspiring story is, at its heart, a tale of refusing to back down.

It's far more difficult to be inspired by someone's accomplishments if there's no indication of hardship. If their daily life seems easy and effortless, it's much harder for us to catch that firefly of inspiration.

Think back to the middle of the pandemic. Although celebrities were locked down and prone to the same virus as the rest of the world, their complaints felt tone deaf. One celebrity posted a video about being quarantined from his NBA regulation–size, private, indoor basketball court. A billionaire wished the world well from his super yacht "isolated in the Grenadines avoiding the virus." Were these celebrities subject to the same lockdowns, fears, and risks as the rest of us? Yes. Did their posts inspire the rest of us that "We're all in this together"? I'd say no.

Hardship is not always visible. Just like an iceberg, our struggles are often happening below the surface. That is, until we're able to rise up out of the water to reach greater heights.

Putting the Framework to Use:

» **Personal:** Name a challenge or setback you've faced. What got you through it, and how are you different because of it? How can that same determination serve you now?

» **Business:** Think of a time your business hit a rough patch. What was the turning point, and what did you learn?

36

AUTHENTICITY

Have you ever found out that a story you loved wasn't true? I'm not talking about Santa Claus or the Easter Bunny. Maybe a memoir hit you just the right way, until you learned it was fiction dressed in nonfiction clothes. It could've been someone you admired who, behind closed doors, was not the person you thought they were. The experience almost feels like betrayal. That's because the third element of an inspirational story displays something deeper than truth—trust. Inspiration requires authenticity.

This third element of an inspiration story shows up in two ways.

The first type of authenticity is veracity, the truth of the story itself. Did this really happen? Are the facts real? The second type of authenticity is alignment. Do I believe this person? Are their words and actions congruent? Is the story they're telling consistent with how they're showing up in the world? Do these match one another?

In 2003, James Frey wrote a memoir about his addiction and road to recovery, *A Million Little Pieces*. Two years later, Oprah Winfrey chose it for her book club and praised it as "so raw and so real." Millions of readers were moved by its gritty honesty.

Until they weren't.

In early 2006, an exposé revealed that many of the details in the book were exaggerated and in some cases, even made up. Oprah invited Frey back on her show and said what many of us were thinking: "I feel duped." Suddenly the glow of inspiration dimmed. Even though the core truths remained, the story's impact was damaged. The container of trust had cracked.

It's happened in sports too. Lance Armstrong inspired millions, not just for winning the Tour de France seven times but for coming back after a brutal cancer diagnosis. The world was astounded at his ability to overcome such adversity, the resilience it took for him to transform his body from post-cancer treatments to the elite athlete he once had been, and the courage it took to get there. His transformation seemed almost miraculous.

Until the doping scandal broke. Suddenly the story of this hero, whom so many had admired for his complete transformation from world-class athlete to cancer patient and back again, wasn't authentic anymore. It didn't feel like a miracle anymore; it felt like a con. And that shift dismantled the emotional architecture of his inspiration.

Authenticity isn't just about what's objectively true. It's also about what we feel to be true. Authenticity breeds belief. As leaders, we may tell our employees a story that's factually true. But if we're sharing those facts and details and our heart isn't in it, or if we don't quite believe it, we'll come off as inauthentic, and our power to inspire implodes. You can have all the facts right, but if your voice, your body language, or your energy betray those facts, people won't honor you with their trust.

Take Marion, a high-ranking executive with a background in politics, who brought the strategic ambiguity so valuable in politics into her corporate leadership. While Marion was beloved by the executive team for her ability to execute on almost any strategy, she wasn't trusted by her peers or subordinates. She earned a reputation for saying one thing and doing another, often operating with a self-serving agenda and an "end justifies the means" mindset.

When a new competitor entered the market with a product that had better features and lower prices, the company quickly lost both revenue and market share. In response, Marion asked her director of sales, Janet, to roll out sweeping changes to the compensation plan. On paper, total earning potential remained the same but only if sales reps dramatically increased their volume and shifted focus to a product that was much more difficult to sell. The company would provide little to no marketing support to drive these new targets.

This was the first breakdown in authenticity. The team didn't believe the "why."

The second breakdown came when Janet pushed the message down the org chart. Because Janet didn't trust in the rationale, her delivery rang hollow. Forced enthusiasm and fake rah-rah always fizzle. The smiles were tight, the delivery was flat, and the employees saw right through it. Instead of motivating the team, the rollout sparked anxiety and speculation, especially whether pay cuts meant that layoffs were next.

A better approach? Janet could have named the discomfort openly with her team. "I know this shift is hard, and I have questions about the rationale. Here's what I do know . . . and how I'm going to advocate for more support for the team . . . Let's talk about how we roll this out with integrity, to manage the fears but also support and encourage the team."

Logically, authenticity is about coherence between the objective elements (Is the story itself true?) and subjective elements (Are the people delivering the message aligned with it?).

Emotionally, the truth is something we feel. It has a frequency we feel in our bones and a special light we can see when people are speaking from their truth. Truth is welcoming. It meets us at the door and helps us slide out of our coats. There is no judgment and no pretense, just presence.

Sometimes the truth is painful, but we see it: a clean bone, the wolf without the sheep's clothing. When we hear a truth we don't like, we may feel bitter or horrified or deeply sad, but I believe our bodies recognize the truth, even when our brains don't.

Authenticity isn't always easy. Authenticity often springs from vulnerability. Being authentic means sharing the cracks, the doubts, the failure and fears—the very things that an inspiring hero overcomes. We want to share the top of the iceberg, not necessarily everything underneath. Yet sometimes the moments we least want to show are the ones that connect us the most.

It's one of the catch-22s about social media. Most people post the highlights of their lives, the trips, the successes, the celebrations. So much of social media is about aspiration, not inspiration. Thousands of accounts regale us with everything from the best ways to lose weight, apply makeup, or redecorate our homes.

That's why aspirational content and inspirational content feel so different. Aspirational content shows us the finished product, whether it's six-pack abs, the designer kitchen, or the sunset from a Santorini rooftop. Inspiration lives in the quiet moment just before: the vulnerability in the voice-over of the athlete struggling with body image, the clutter beyond the photo frame of that designer kitchen, the burned-out exec thinking about how tired they are before stepping out on that rooftop.

Elyse Myers is a great example of a content creator who has embraced both adversity and authenticity in her rise to fame. As a writer and comedian with millions of followers, she built her following by recounting hilarious, awkward, and sometimes deeply painful moments from her life. She's spoken openly about ADHD, autism, body image, imposter syndrome, and anxiety. She's wildly imperfect, but that's why millions of people love and trust her. Those imperfections feel familiar, and her stories feel true.

Authenticity may not be polished, but it feels right. And that matters a lot in regard to inspiration.

One of my clients posted gorgeous wedding photos on social media—big smiles and joy all around. A week later, he told me his son had been bitten by a dog the morning of the wedding. There was an emergency room visit, stitches, fear, and some PTSD. None of that was included in the photos. To be clear, I'm not criticizing his choice. The example highlights the fact that what we see isn't always the truth. Real life includes shadows. We forget that what truly inspires us isn't perfection; it's realness, effort, and resilience.

Authenticity reminds us that the headline is not the whole story, and behind every accomplishment lies doubt, detour, and dark nights of the soul.

Inspiration doesn't just depend on facts so much as faith. Sometimes even when a story has been disproven, if a person's belief in the "hero" is still intact, the story can continue to inspire them. That's why authenticity matters. It's a bridge between story and soul, and it allows someone else's experience to spark a fire for us.

Putting the Framework to Use:

» **Personal:** Recall a moment when you showed up as your true self. What did you risk, and what did you gain? How can your true self help you now, in whatever situation you are facing?

» **Business:** Identify a time your organization chose values over convenience. How was that decision made? What was lost and gained as a result of that choice? How did it affect trust or culture?

37

RESILIENCE

We often celebrate the big, bold moments, the dramatic acts of heroism that make headlines. We are wowed by the singular acts of courage: the mom who lifts a car off her toddler, someone who pushes a stranger out of the path of an oncoming bus, the person who tackles an active shooter at a shopping mall. These moments of great strength, bravery, or selflessness are impressive, even awe-inspiring. We can celebrate them, but because the actions are one-time events and often unrepeatable, they rarely move us to action.

The kind of inspiration that sparks something inside of us and makes us want to try, to begin, to change comes from something quieter and more consistent: resilience. Resilience isn't about saving someone from a burning building. It's getting up and doing the hard thing again and again, even when no one is watching. It's taking the firefighter's test, failing, then taking it again so you can save someone's life. Resilience transforms admiration into action. In the most inspirational stories, resilience clears the path between hardship and hope.

Resilience is the fourth pillar of an inspirational story. It's the quiet, steady force behind transformation. Inspiration doesn't require perfection, but it does require persistence. Resilience is similar to grit, and as Angela Duckworth writes in her book *Grit,*

"To be gritty is to keep putting one foot in front of the other. To be gritty is to hold fast to an interesting and purposeful goal. To be gritty is to invest, day after week after year, in challenging practice. To be gritty is to fall down seven times, and rise eight."

Resilience shows up in the person who's struggling to live a healthier lifestyle and comes to a class at the gym for the first time, and we can see how hard it is for them. We might feel sympathy or empathy for that person while remembering our first day in a spin class, lifting weights, or walking on the treadmill.

But we see that person showing up every day to make a change. They post videos on social media of their daily trip to the gym and their workouts. They talk about learning to have a different relationship with food, and they are eating healthier, they're sleeping more, drinking more water, making different choices. Living a new life. Sometimes they have setbacks. They don't have time to make a healthy dinner or got caught late at a stressful day at work and ended up getting a pizza. We empathize with those moments too—adversity lends greater authenticity to their journey. The next day, they're back at the gym, back to eating well, back to their dedication to reaching their goals. When someone shows persistence and resilience, especially over a long period of time, it reminds us that our goals are possible, that we can do it too.

Resilience doesn't always look like grit-your-teeth toughness. Sometimes it looks like gentleness or grace. It can even look like crawling when you want to run.

Take the story of David, a middle-aged man who came to me wanting to "become a writer." The challenge? He was reading and writing at an elementary school level. He hadn't read a book in years but had a lot of heart, which mattered more than any book he could have read. We started with the basics, identifying different parts of speech and simple sentence construction. I introduced him to *The Artist's Way* by Julia Cameron, and he started writing morning pages every day. Three pages, without judgment, just words.

He filled journal after journal. He devoured every writing exercise. I gave him tough feedback and he took it. I gave him reading lists, and he read novels and short stories, poetry and plays. David was working two jobs. But he came back and revised drafts of what he'd written. When he got stuck in the story he was writing, he got frustrated, but he came back to the page. Over time, his characters came alive and his language evolved. And one day, a few years later, David held a copy of a local anthology that contained his published short story.

That's the power of resilience.

David's story isn't flashy, perhaps not worthy of a movie montage. It's real, and it speaks to anyone who has doubted themselves, stepped far outside their comfort zone, or wondered if they were too far behind, too old, or too underqualified. That's what makes it profoundly inspiring.

We often romanticize persistence and resilience in professional athletes, and rightly so. They overcome extreme physical challenges and continue to perform at the very highest levels. In 2006, after experiencing fatigue and back pain, twenty-two-year-old Red Sox pitcher Jon Lester was diagnosed with anaplastic large-cell lymphoma, a rare form of blood cancer. He began chemotherapy immediately and missed the rest of the season.

Most people would have hung up their cleats, but not Jon Lester. Eleven months after his diagnosis, he returned to the mound. Not only did he resume his career, but he thrived. In 2007, he started and won the World Series–clinching game for Boston. The following year he pitched a no-hitter against Kansas City.

He went on to become a five-time All-Star and won three World Series titles across three teams. It's not just his stats that inspire us, it's his story. It's the daily, unseen effort to come back after chemo, the discipline and mental fortitude, and most of all, his belief that cancer wasn't the end of his story.

Every Olympic athlete is an example of resilience. We're inspired not just by the medal ceremony and the incredible feats of strength and athleticism. We're inspired by what they represent: years of training, early mornings, late evenings, stringent routines, strict diets, setbacks, injuries, disappointments, failures. And the daily decision to continue toward their dreams. To pay the price for what they want.

Resilience isn't a single moment; it's a pattern and a posture. It's a commitment to keep showing up even when the odds are against you. It stretches beyond survival stories and sports. It lives in our everyday lives: the parent learning to show up differently for their kid, the leader rebuilding trust with their team, the artist continuing to create behind closed doors.

Resilience helps us transmute hope into faith.

Because when we see someone try, fall down, and then get back up again, over and over, we don't just admire them. We believe in them. And that helps us believe in ourselves too.

Putting the Framework to Use:

» **Personal:** Write about a time you kept going when it would have been easier to quit. What fueled you?

» **Business:** Recall a challenge your organization persisted through. What habits or systems made that possible?

38

TRANSFORMATION

Powerful stories aren't just about what happened but what *changed*. A person became someone new, either on the outside or the inside. An idea cracked open to reveal an entirely new direction. A worldview was upended, which allowed for healing and peace.

Transformation is the fifth and final pillar of an inspirational story. Transformation is the caterpillar becoming the butterfly. It's the moment Simone Biles reclaims the mat, not just as an elite athlete but as a fierce advocate for mental health. It's Sara Blakely, founder and CEO of Spanx, cutting the feet off of pantyhose in her apartment with $5,000 and no business experience and turning the idea into a billion-dollar business. It's also the patient ringing the bell for their last chemo treatment. It's the employee who finally sets a boundary with their boss after years of staying silent.

People may be transformed physically. A person loses the weight or finishes the race. They leave a job or a relationship. There's something we can see. But the most significant shifts happen inside, whether it's a new perspective, quiet courage, or a change in our own values or ideas.

Transformations may be big and public. Oprah Winfrey was born into poverty in rural Mississippi. She endured abuse, teen pregnancy, and deep instability before her rise to global influence. Oprah is now worth an estimated $3 billion, but her transformation is about more than fame or fortune. It's about becoming a force for empathy, literacy, wellness, and possibility. Her life shifted not only her own trajectory, but millions of other people have been energized and moved—and inspired—by her example.

Quiet, everyday transformations show up in a lesson learned, a change in perspective, a new rule to live by based on an experience you've lived through. You see examples of this every day, whether people experience the death of a loved one, a divorce, losing a job, or even moving to another country. They learn that grief is not linear, or that conflict avoidance can be worse than actual conflict. They learn that losing a job isn't always about failure and that doing something in a new way can make them stronger and more patient.

When you ask someone to name the person that inspires them most, they often mention a family member, a parent or grandparent. The mom who never missed a birthday, who showed up with soup while we were sick, who worked three jobs without ever complaining. The granddad who always stood up for the underdog, who helped heal those around him with humor, who always went out of his way to make people feel welcome and included. They rarely describe that family member becoming a different person but will say instead, "That's just who they always were." Sometimes we're not inspired by a person who changed but by a person who remains steadfast. Those people didn't transform themselves—they transformed us.

How critical is transformation to inspiration? What if you saw someone experience adversity with authenticity, courage, and persistence, and yet nothing changed as a result? What if Ebenezer Scrooge spent his evening with the ghost of past, present, and future only to wake up the same cranky and cantankerous soul? How inspired would we be by the story of *A Christmas Carol*?

Seeing transformation in other people allows us to see that change is possible for us. The transformation we witness becomes the permission slip for ourselves.

Maybe you struggle with controlling your anger, or have difficulty speaking up for yourself. You may wish that you were more laid back and less anxious, or less scattered and more focused. You may aspire to be a better parent, a better sibling, a better spouse, a better leader or employee, or a better community member. People who inspire us show us we can be less angry or have more confidence. They give us the example of how we can make an incremental shift in how we treat people or how we show up in our lives.

Inspiration is about hope and possibility, of limitlessness. It's about seeing what we could achieve. In inspiring stories, the protagonist is never saved—they save themselves. And we can too.

The people who inspire us show us what's possible. They give us a blueprint or a spark. Sometimes they even light the match that sets our transformation in motion.

Inspiration gives us a feeling of transcendence, of rising above or touching something beyond the ordinary. Transformation is what happens next. It's the new shape we take and the new story we live.

Putting the Framework to Use:

- » **Personal:** Think of a time you became a different version of yourself. What sparked the change, and what's better now?

- » **Business:** Identify a major transformation your organization has undergone. What triggered it, and what's the lasting impact?

AFTERWORD

You've made it to the end of the book, and in many ways, the beginning. A potentially new beginning for how you see yourself, your leadership, and the sparks you carry forward.

Throughout these pages, we've explored inspiration: what it is, how it works, and how to cultivate it. We've looked at what it takes to ignite it in yourself and others, to tell richer stories, to lead more boldly and live more fully.

So now I'll leave you with this:

You don't have to be famous to be inspirational. You don't need a platform or a viral story, or a grand, cinematic life.

You just have to be human.

To show up honestly. To keep going when it's hard. To choose courage when fear whispers in your ear. To stay the course when it would be easier to quit. To not only let inspiration move though you but transform you in the process.

When you do, your story—ordinary or extraordinary, quiet or loud—just might become the spark that lights someone else's way.

So go ahead.

Go light the fire.

ACKNOWLEDGEMENTS

This book exists because of an incredible constellation of people who showed up for me with brilliance, patience, encouragement, and love.

To Anne Janzer, coach, cheerleader, thought partner, book doula, and writer—this book would not exist without you. Your wisdom and steady presence lit the path.

To Carla Green, thank you for the cover that stopped me in my tracks the first time I saw it. You gave this book its first spark of life visually, and I am endlessly grateful.

To Danielle Devening-Limon, who somehow makes sense of my crazy brain, thank you for translating my ideas into a stunning website and for walking beside me in the marketing journey.

To Laurie Gibson, for bravely editing a second book of mine and to Kim Bookless, for your brilliant proofreading and eye for detail. You've both made this book stronger, sharper, and clearer.

To my Vistage Chair colleagues, your encouragement carried me. To Bill Kern, Darrell Jackson, and Terry Buske—the Quad Squad—for keeping tabs on my daily word counts with good humor and accountability. To the Monday crew—Mark Fackler, Mike Malone, Alan Sorkin, and Jim Heaton—for grounding me when I most needed it. And to my faculty team, Linda Gabbard, Irina Baranov, Niels Lameijer, Rick Schleufer, Lance Descourouez, Lauryn Rice, Bob Dabic, and Nancy Girres, you inspire me every day to stretch, to serve, and to love.

To my Vistage members, your stories, courage, and curiosity are the heartbeat of this work. The love and leadership you bring to your organizations, communities, and the world inspire me more than words can say. Thank you for the gift of letting me serve you.

To my friends who encouraged me in countless moments: Miné Okano, Gillian Dunn, Jen Horton, Jenny Graham, Laurie King, Jocelyn Kessler, Cristy Houk, Kristen Fogle, Paige Nolan, Megan Tupa, Alessandra Wall, Rekha Chandrabose, Abbie Nickel, Laura Furness, Katie Wagner, and Mariel Diaz, thank you for reminding me I wasn't alone in this. Writing this feels a little like giving an Oscars speech where the music swells and I know I'm forgetting people. Please know my deepest gratitude extends beyond this list to every person who nudged, challenged, or believed in me during this journey. You may not see your name here, but you are written into these pages all the same.

To Dad, Nikki, Eric, Jacque, Madison, Hannah, and Emily—thank you for loving me through the chaos, cheering me through the chapters, and reminding me every day that you are my greatest joy and my truest inspiration.

And finally, to you, the reader. The most precious thing we have in this life besides love is time. Thank you for spending some of yours with me and this book. My hope is that something here lights a spark for you, one you can carry into your own life and the lives of those around you.

NOTES AND CITATIONS

Every spark has tinder. What follows are the sparks behind the sparks—the research, stories, and references that fueled this book. If you want to go deeper, wander through these notes and see where the trail leads.

CHAPTER 2: WHY INSPIRATION MATTERS

Bain & Company conducted a study: This study was cited in a *Harvard Business Review* article: "Engaging Your Employees Is Good, But Don't Stop There," by Eric Garten and Michael Mankins, *Harvard Business Review* (December 9, 2015), https://hbr.org/2015/12/engaging -your-employees-is-good-but-dont-stop-there.

CHAPTER 5: MOTIVATION VS. INSPIRATION

Stephen Covey's "Be-Do-Have" framework: Stephen R. Covey, *The 7 Habits of Highly Effective People: Powerful Lessons in Personal Change* (New York: Free Press, 1989).

CHAPTER 6: THE WONDER TWINS AT WORK

In one last example, a colleague was struggling: For more on the Avoider Saboteur, read Shirzad Chamine's *Positive Intelligence: Why Only 20% of Teams and Individuals Achieve Their True Potential and How You Can Achieve Yours* (Greenleaf Book Group Press, 2012).

CHAPTER 12: THE ART OF RUTHLESS PRIORITIZATION

One of my favorite prioritization methods is the Eisenhower matrix: Stephen R. Covey, *The 7 Habits of Highly Effective People: Powerful Lessons in Personal Change* (New York: Free Press, 1989).

In James Patterson's book: James Patterson, *Suzanne's Diary for Nicholas* (Little, Brown, and Company, 2001).

CHAPTER 15: PERMISSION SLIPS

In Braving the Wilderness: Find the permission slip exercise in Brené Brown's *Braving the Wilderness: The Quest for True Belonging and the Courage to Stand Alone* (New York: Random House, 2017).

CHAPTER 16: LETTING GO

Suleika Jaouad, the bestselling author and creator of *The Isolation Journals*: *The Isolation Journals* is a newsletter and online community, accessible at https://www.theisolationjournals.com/.

CHAPTER 18: THE CATHEDRAL EFFECT

Researchers studied the influence of ceiling height: Joan Meyers-Levy and Rui Zhu, "The Influence of Ceiling Height: The Effect of Priming on the Type of Processing That People Use," *Journal of Consumer Research* 34, no. 2 (August 2007): 174–186, https://doi.org/10.1086/519146.

In one of his podcast episodes: Andrew Huberman, "Optimizing Workspace for Productivity, Focus, & Creativity," *Huberman Lab Podcast*, January 31, 2022.

CHAPTER 19: THE GREAT OUTDOORS EFFECT

In his book *A Year in the Woods*: Torbjørn Ekelund, *A Year in the Woods: Twelve Small Journeys into Nature*, translated by Becky L. Crook (Greystone Books, 2021).

Plenty of research ties the awe of nature to creativity: Paul K. Piff, Pia Dietze, Matthew Feinberg, Daniel M. Stancato, and Dacher Keltner, "Awe, the Small Self, and Prosocial Behavior," *Journal of Personality and Social Psychology* 108, no. 6 (2015): 883–899, https://doi.org/10.1037/pspi0000018.

CHAPTER 20: BRING THE OUTSIDE IN

During the pandemic, houseplant sales grew: Statista Research Department cited a 2021 expenditure of £7.6 billion, up 18 percent from 2020. "Annual expenditure on plants and flowers in the United Kingdom, 2021," *Statista* (2023), https://www.cladco.co.uk/blog/post/uk-gardening-statistics.

Research shows that even small doses of nature: Jee Heon Rhee, Brian Schermer, Gisung Han, So Yeon Park, and Kyung Hoon Lee, "Effects of Nature on Restorative and Cognitive Benefits in Indoor Environment," *Scientific Reports* 13 (2023): Article 13199.

CHAPTER 21: THE ART OF MENTAL STILLNESS

In his book *Stillness Is the Key*: For a deep, thoughtful exploration of stillness, see Ryan Holiday's books *Stillness Is the Key* (Portfolio, 2019) and *The Daily Stoic* (Portfolio, 2016).

CHAPTER 22: DON'T FEAR THE VOID

A study conducted at University of California, San Francisco: Timothy D. Wilson, David A. Reinhard, Erin C. Westgate, Daniel T. Gilbert, Nicole Ellerbeck, Cheryl Hahn, Casey L. Brown, and Adi Shaked, "Just Think: The Challenges of the Disengaged Mind," *Science* 345, no. 6192 (July 4 2014): 75–77, https://doi.org/10.1126/science.1250830.

Several studies show the correlation between smartphone use and increased stress and emotional dysregulation: Here are two of them. Sharon Horwood and Jeromy Anglim, "Emotion Regulation Difficulties, Personality, and Problematic Smartphone Use," *Cyberpsychology, Behavior, and Social Networking,* 24, no. 4 (2021): 275–281, https://doi.org/10.1089/cyber.2020.0328.

Jinwoo Cho & Hoyoung Kim, "The Role of Impulsivity and Emotional Dysregulation in Smartphone Overdependence Explored Through Network Analysis," *Scientific Reports* 15, no. 1852 (2025), https://doi.org/10.1038/s41598-025-85680-1.

CHAPTER 24: QUIETING THE JUDGE

In his book *The War of Art*: Steven Pressfield, *The War of Art* (Rugged Land, 2002).

CHAPTER 26: STILLNESS IN MOTION

A study published in January of 2024 suggested that low-frequency noise: Peng Liang, Jiangjing Li, Zenglei Li, Jing Wei, Jing Li, Shenghao Zhang, Shenglong Xu, Zhaohui Liu, and Jin Wang, "Effect of Low-Frequency Noise Exposure on Cognitive Function: A Systematic Review and Meta-Analysis," *BMC Public Health* 24 (2024): 125, https://doi.org/10.1186/s12889-023-17593-5.

CHAPTER 27: IMAGINATION AS INSPIRATION FUEL

There is so much science around visualization: Katrina Volgemute, Zermena Vazne, Romualdas Malinauskas, "The Benefits of Guided Imagery on Athletic Performance," *Frontiers in Psychology* Apr 11, no. 16 (2025): 1500194, https://www.frontiersin.org/journals/psychology/articles/10.3389/fpsyg.2025.1500194.

CHAPTER 29: THE COLLECTIVE SPARK

Priya Parker wrote a gorgeous book: Priya Parker, *The Art of Gathering* (Riverhead Books, 2018).

CHAPTER 30: WHEN NATURE MAKES YOU FORGET YOURSELF

A 2015 Stanford study found that walking in nature: Gregory N. Bratman, J. Paul Hamilton, Kevin S. Hahn, Gretchen C. Daily, and James J. Gross, "Nature Experience Reduces Rumination and Subgenual Prefrontal Cortex Activation," *Proceedings of the National Academy of Sciences of the United States of America* 112, no. 28 (2015): 8567–8572, https://doi.org/10.1073/pnas.1510459112.

But awe does more than just clear away our mental clutter: Here are two great studies about the power of awe. Paul K. Piff, Pia Dietze, Matthew Feinberg, Daniel M. Stancato, and Dacher Keltner, "Awe, the 'Small Self,' and Pro-social Behavior," *Journal of Personality and Social Psychology* 108, no. 6 (2015): 883–899, https://doi.org/10.1037/pspi0000018.

Maria Monroy and Dacher Keltner, "Awe as a Pathway to Mental and Physical Health," *Perspectives on Psychological Science* 18, no. 2 (2023): 350–365, https://doi.org/10.1177/17456916221094856.

CHAPTER 31: ART

A study from Cambridge University in 2025: Fred Lewsey, "Pondering Artistic Beauty Encourages 'Big Picture' Thinking," *University of Cambridge*, May 7, 2025, https://www.cam.ac.uk/stories/artistic-beauty-abstract-thinking.

In *The Art of Noticing*: Rob Walker, *The Art of Noticing* (Knopf, 2019).

CHAPTER 32: FLEXIBLE DISCIPLINE

In *Atomic Habits*, James Clear does a beautiful job: James Clear, *Atomic Habits* (Avery, 2018).

CHAPTER 33: THE INSPIRATION CHART

Research by the psychologists at York University: Raymond A. Mar, Jingyuan Li, Anh T. P. Nguyen & Cindy Ta, "Memory and Comprehension of Narrative Versus Expository Texts: A Meta-Analysis." *Psychonomic Bulletin & Review* 28, 732-749 (2023), https://doi.org/10.3758/s13423-020-01853-1.

CHAPTER 37: RESILIENCE

Resilience is similar to grit: Angela Duckworth, *Grit: The Power of Passion and Perseverance* (Scribner, 2016).